Reason "N" Rap

Spiritual Motivation for Life Performance

Pastor Henry O. Hardy

McClure Publishing, Inc.

ISBN-13: 978-0-9989223-5-5

Cover Design by Kathy McClure

Photographer – Carey Borders

To order additional copies, please contact:
McClure Publishing, Inc.
www.mcclurepublishing.com
800.659.4908

FOREWORD

The purpose of this book is to enunciate positive motivational principles for dynamic Christian living. It is designed for poetic and motivational inspiration. We are aware of unusual sentence structure and grammatical uniqueness. It is designed, for you, the reader to experience the "Rhythm of the Rhyme and let your heart feel the beat." The effort grows out of my observation of contemporary culture and the dominant role played by what is termed the 'hip hop and rap' generation. This phenomenon had its coming out party as a rhyming mixture of words couched in a musical cadence. The attraction of this genre is enhanced by its emphasis on performance encouraging its listeners to get in sync with its beat.

The rap syndrome is often characterized by an earthy and sometimes profane nature. Much of the lyrics could not be performed in polite company and definitely not in a conventional worship setting.

But its tremendous popularity led me to think that there could be a positive message conveyed by this "rap" idiom. I wanted to communicate that Christ is relevant and that His message is meaningful. I decided to write some rap essays for performance at my church. These pieces were perspectives on love, justice, faith, prayer, and the like.

The "Reason-N-Rap" style is designed to encourage reflection. It is hoped that the reading of these meditations will result in "life performance" – a change in how we respond to life situations. The purpose of the rhyming technique is to cause one to rhythmically respond to God conscious and Christ centered ideas so that the motivated reader will say: YES, I can do that!

It is my desire to rehearse what my late mentor, Dr. D.E. King, one of the nation's most profound preachers, termed "take home pay." He felt that one should benefit from participating in the worship experience. It is my hope that this book will provide similar spiritual and religious nurture.

The "rap" of this work may be defined thusly:

"Time to live on a higher plane / Let our witness defeat the profane"

This is the season for "life performance and demonstration" of our faith. The mission of this book is that of an urgent voice singing a new song. I trust that the depth and delight of this effort will have lasting benefits – long after the latest "hip hop" award show has faded into dusty oblivion.

This motivational testament is not only drawn in the rap and rhyming style but is a "map" for creative living. I trust that you will join with those who are the believers in this book's message – and go into "all the world" with the commission to make it better. And things get better when we perform better in life.

Pastor Henry O. Hardy
February 14, 2018

DEDICATION

I am indebted to those who provided oxygen and inspiration on the journey of this book's completion. Your consciousness and assistance gave buoyancy to my efforts in coping with the pregnancy of the creative process. It is my hope that what has been birthed will be radiant revelation on the path to spiritual discovery.

Henry O. Hardy

Table of Contents

BE A BELIEVER!

FINISH WHAT YOU STARTED

Let Your Light So Shine

Love

Mountains Are Made For Climbing

The World Is At Your Fingertips

Spiritual Motivation

For

Life Performance

"THE AWESOMENESS OF GOD"

GOD, YOU ARE AMAZING

Let all the earth fear the Lord: let all the Inhabitants of the world stand in awe of him
Psalm 33:8 (KJV)

Amazing is His definition / Answer for my condition / A God who never fails / Comfort when the storm wails / Holds me in His arm / My shelter from harm / Keeps an eye on my travels / Provides when my condition unravels / A strength that won't falter / I can bring it to the altar / Give Him my plight / No need for fright / He chases the night / Surrounds me with light / He's a wonder in action / Really is the main attraction / Enables me to gain speed / Nurtures and fulfills my need / God is truly great / Essence of a soul mate / His love is never late / He really is the best date / God is more than I can express / He's there in my test / All my failures notwithstanding / Guides my flight to a safe landing / Watches my going and coming / Now, that's really something / Gives me escort service / No reason to be nervous / Holds my hand as I walk / Enlightened by God talk / His eyes are never blind / I'm always on His mind / It's life changing stuff / Support when it's tough / He is true and real / Always will close the deal / Counsels me to stay on point / He will protect and anoint / Abides under His care / Never fails to share / Better with Him at my side / Ability that can't be denied / A peace chasing the doubt / He's always the "look out" / Always there when I call / Never touring the mall / My life is so much better / No trial I can't weather / It's all because of His love / Mastery sent from above/ Firms my confidence in my trial / It's good to be His child / Got the proof of divine relief / Prize for my belief / God just wants my trust / He is ever just / Lifts me from the dust / Holds me secure and sure / It's His promise that I can endure / Just be still and witness / God provides spirit and fitness / Gives me the boost for the trip / His vigilance won't let me slip / God is really the "last word" / Trusting anything else is absurd / Amen /

IMPOSSIBILITY IS ATTEMPTING TO ASSIGN LIMITATIONS TO GOD.

THE WONDER OF GOD

Sing forth the honour of his name: make his praise glorious.
Psalm 66:2 (KJV)

You are the God for all seasons / The rhythm for my dissonance / The relief for my grief / The peace for my conflict / The light for my darkness / The hope for my extremity / The deliverance from my distress / The rescue from crisis / The joy for my sorrow / The tenderness in the turbulence / The understanding in confusion / The shield in my struggle / The bridge over the abyss / The gentling for my hurt / The wisdom for my way / The patience for my fretfulness / The comfort for my pain / The assurance for my anxiety / The solution for my problem / The conquest in challenge / The whisper in the storm / The refuge for my wandering / The acceptance for my rejection / The strength for my weakness / The reward for my service / The insight for my ignorance / The smile in the furor / The food for my hunger / The water for my thirst / The rain for desert times / The meaning in my seeking / The elevation in desperation / The companion in my travels. The laughter in my tears / The nurturer of my dreams / The defender in my trial / The wonder in the weariness / The liberation from limitation / The watcher for my walk / The oxygen for the race / The prosperity for my adversity / The security in my dwelling / The sentry for my sleep /

The presence in my present / You are the God for all seasons /

GOD IS WONDERFUL!
DON'T EMBRACE BEING AVERAGE.

GOD IS

The Lord is my light and my salvation; whom shall I fear?
Psalm 27:1a (KJV)

My God is my guide / Leads me and stays by my side / Always seeks to protect / Patient even when I defect / Considers me His child / Never fails to handle me tender and mild / Glad I know the Man / His compassion always lends a hand / God is light in the night / Vision that chases the fright / Just look to God for all I need / Truly is my supply indeed / God is! God is! / Can't deny that sometimes I get leery / Body tired and my soul teary / But God spans space to touch me / Bonding with Him is divine, you see / All things work according to His will / He supplies power to climb the hill / Just hang in for goodness sake / Victory is mine for what I can take / There is no defeat in prayer / God's presence is always there / I obey the Master's plan / Join in and hold His hand / Going forward and won't turn around / On my way to higher ground / Coming up rough trails / Not worried - He never fails / Keeping my eyes lifted up / It's His grace that drank the cup / Confident that I got it made / His answers make the grade / Never stop believing in God's power / Always there in every hour / Going on with persistence / I got the victory despite resistance / No way that I can lose / God's resources are what I use / So renew your hope / Refuse to mope

/ Begin to cope / It's a comfort to tell you / He'll see you through / Backing up my plan / Hey, He's the man / God is! God is! /

GOD IS NEVER NOT "IS." I AM BECAUSE GOD IS.

GOD'S OUTLINE

In all thy ways acknowledge him, and he shall direct thy paths.
Proverbs 3:6 (KJV)

Plans are put on hold / Under pressure to fold / Easy to drop out and die / Life's more than a sigh / Victory is given to the strong of heart / Those not afraid to start / Just reach for the trip chart / Follow God's scheme without fear / He's not distant, but near / Always stands at the ready / His balance keeps us steady / Holds us when we would fall / Ever waiting for our call / Desires that we succeed / There to meet every need / Reaches us in stress / Offers grace for the test / No one cares like God / Always consistent - never odd / Looks out when storms brew / Offers us a brighter view / Waits for us to be still / All our requests can be filled / God's there to bless / Patient when we get in a mess / No reason to doubt / God can bring us out / Best path is His map / Always close, spanning the gap / His grace carries the day / Assurance that He'll make a way / Just be resolute and stay / Right where we are / God is the brightest star / No need for despair / God's in charge of repair / Things will be fine / God is awesome and divine / It's no cause to shiver / God can and will deliver / His book is the Code / Really our rules of the road / We have the plan / Bring peace to the land / Wait upon Ezekiel's wheel / Our God's not run of the mill /

Promises to redeem us from sin / His game plan is sure to win / Sure to win /

GOD'S INSTRUCTION ENABLES YOU TO AVOID DESTRUCTION

GOD CAN

I can do all things through Christ which strengtheneth me.
Philippians 4:13 (KJV)

When the way is dark / Hope gone - missed the mark / Keep your grip tight / God's got you in his sight / Believe that you can win / Refuse to whimper and give in / God can do great stuff / Always for you when it's rough / Never has failed to hear the cry / Just know He'll stop by / No way you are alone / God's faithful to the bone / All things work in His will / God's got you – that's the deal / Hold your head high / Believe and don't sigh / No defeat in His name / You can beat the game / Start your day with hope / God's able – you can cope / Things will be fine / Never forget God's on line / It's your victory you know / Trials only let you grow / Your day is not sour / God's love covers your hour / Act bold and walk tall / Surely there's God if you hit the wall / Plan for victory is God's / His love beats the odds / Trust in the Savior / Closer than a neighbor / So keep a steady pace / God's full of grace / Smiles on his face / Stay in the race / God can handle trouble / Holds you on the bubble / Be certain it's alright/ Safe passage from night to light / God can right the wrong / Keep looking up – sing your song / Do it strong – all the day long / Where trials try to stop/ Your place is at the top / Despite conflict in the land / God can! God can! /

REACH FOR GOD'S HAND. HE IS ARTHRITIS FREE!

GOD'S ON DUTY

Behold, He that keepeth Israel shall neither slumber nor sleep.

Psalm 121:4 (KJV)

God has something for you / No reason to be blue / Just believe in His power / Comes through hour after hour / His will is for your success / Wants you to have the best / It's a matter of belief / Recipe for relief / His grace is unfailing / Quiets all woe and wailing / Keeps watching your going / It's all about your growing / His promise is sure / Its faith that'll endure / God's love covers your path / Overcomes the devil's wrath / Puts to flight his plot / Better than "Johnny on the spot" / God is on the throne / He's closer than your phone / Call him at any time / Don't even need a dime / Just dial His number / He's never known to slumber / Gives you special attention / That's worth a mention / His response is your joy / God is direct and never coy / Comes to lift the load / Constant in his help mode / His assistance has no strings / Available whatever life brings / He's a wonder you can trust / Always caring and just / You don't have to doubt / God's never been counted out / You are in the safety zone / Never left alone / Get your mind in gear / There's nothing to fear / God's "got your back" / And your "front" wont lack / He covers better than paint / His vigilance doesn't faint / You can embrace this day / Just walk in the God way /

Trust your plan to advance / God's touch will enhance / Give a "shout out" to God / He's the shepherd with the strong rod / Supports you with his staff / He's truly a life raft /

RELAX! GOD'S GOT HIS EYES ON YOU!

GOD DESERVES IT

Enter into his gates with thanksgiving,
and into his courts with praise: be thankful unto him,
and bless his name.
Psalm 100:4 (KJV)

God never puts us down / Give Him a smile – no frown / Least we can do is offer a clap / He puts us on life's map / Brought us here by His will / Now that's a sweet deal / Gave us a mind to reason / Always with us from season to season / Offers the fragrance of Spring / Allows our souls to sing / Summer time for kids to play / Laughter filling the day / Winter with its snow / Glistening with a crystal glow / Autumn sharing its leafy beauty / Giving praise is easy duty / What a world where we live / God's always willing to give / All things are here for us / An expression of God's trust / It's ours to protect / Pollution is a folly to reject / Blesses us with His provision / Giving thanks is the right decision / All things come through His grace / Ingratitude is such a waste / Too hurried for God acclaim / Now that's a shame / Consider who is our Source / Sufficiency for life's course / Always present to give aid / Not looking to get paid / Loves to offer kindness / Ingratitude is a blindness /Acting like we are doing it on our own / Such views are error prone / Time to give God "props" / He's first and always "tops" / It's His eyes upon us / Created from His dust / We spring from the Genesis vault / Denying it is our fault / Worshipping the world is the wrong obsession / Fearing Him is the right profession / Putting God in our devotion / That's wisdom in motion / All about lifting His name / No cause for shame / Must not carry faith at half-mast / It's a farce that won't last / Offer God praise and applause / Never put Him on pause / Our life comes from Him / Fills our cups to the brim / His power is never reduced / Offers more pep than our morning juice / Give a shout out to His name / Glory to God / He's the creator of the game /

WHAT IS THERE TO SAY? GOD SAYS IT ALL!

GOD IS AVAILABLE

..., My presence shall go with thee,...
Exodus 33:14 (KJV)

Seems we keep on messing up / Drinking from the error cup / Leaning to our human vision / Treating God with derision / Better wise up and learn / God's mind is the right turn / Putting our hope in Him / There when we are on a limb / Yet we keep acting crazy / Like our eyesight is hazy / Why we do what we do / Always choosing the vanity view / Interest in money and honey / That makes our day sunny / We don't ever realize / Takes more than things to actualize / Called to be wise keepers / Fate can't rest in sleepers / Must emerge with insight / Have a plan from morning to night / Got to get our act in gear / Find a way when it's drear / Trusting God is not queer / Perfect love chases fear / This is the day God made / What's our grade / Did we pass or fail / Choose truth to tell / Our hope must not waver / God provides favor / Change for better is the solution / End the mind pollution / Act with resolution / Start the revolution / Call on strength inside / It's the Lord who'll provide / His power is ours / A help when program sours / Wise to put God first / He's there when time is worst / Never runs out in trouble / Rescues us from the rubble / Lifts us from a low state / On time and never late / Holds us in His strength /

Stays with us despite the length / Seems like a wiser move / Discover depth of the God groove / It's His skill in trouble shooting / God deserves our rooting / Giving Him praise for His acts / Clear there's nothing He lacks / No other scheme gives peace / God grants prison release / Freed from mind cuffs / Only vanity huffs and puffs / What a blessing in His Word / Confident our prayer is heard / No excuse for going it alone / God sits on the throne / The Lord provides / His power presides / It's His joy in sharing / Lets relax and enjoy His caring /

YOU ARE ON GOD'S SCHEDULE.
TAKE ADVANTAGE OF IT!

THE LORD IS MY SHEPHERD

The Lord is my shepherd; I shall not want.
Psalm 23:1 (KJV)

His rod and staff never fail / Protection over hill and dale / Vigil through the valley / God's angels keep tally / Got to keep the pasture / Be open to the Master / Know that wolves come to destroy / Yet my faith I must employ / Put it in God's control / Doing it alone will take its toll / Believe that God knows best / Will do more - not less / Can lead through the mess / Help you win the test / The Lord is my guide / It's His wealth He'll provide / Just trust and decide / Believe God and don't hide / The Shepherd knows where to go / His path has a bright glow / His will is no joke / He's there when I am broke / God knows the map / Leads around gulleys and gaps / His strength is my resource / It's my armed force / Puts to flight danger to sheep / Calms the waters - dark and deep / Really is on top of His game / No need to murmur and blame / God would not fool us / His essence is pure trust / Stand your ground / He has you sized for a crown / Think of what you will behold / Safe in His fold / Dwelling in the Lord's house / His light is never doused / Home at last / Reward for holding fast / God is a good host / Worthy of the highest toast / He's the Best Deal / Comfort in His will / The Lord really keeps the sheep / No cause to weep / Just got to sing the song / The Shepherd King does it strong! /

GOD'S WATCHING YOU! HE WON'T LEAVE YOU TO FIGHT THE WOLFPACK BY YOURSELF.

NO FAILURE IN GOD

I had fainted, unless I had believed to see the goodness of the LORD in the land of the living.
Psalm 27:13 (KJV)

It's all about conviction / In life, that's a benediction / Standing on a platform / Don't have to conform / Chosen to make God proud / Say it loud / God has His eye on me / It's about what I see / No time to live in a rut / Can't seek refuge in a "but" / Have to assume my role / Must score the goal / The game is on / Good to know the Son / Strength that endures / A love that assures / All things under His power / He's our high tower / Held in His grace / Stamina for the race / Running strong for the crown / No cause to frown / Looking toward the finish line / God is one of a kind / Gives me joy in my striving / Helps me in my driving / Going forward with zeal / Christ is real / Leave behind the doubt load / He is Master of the life road / Assurance that it's okay / Jesus declares He is the way /

RELIEVE YOUR ACHING BACK.
GIVE YOUR BURDENS TO THE LORD.

TRANSFORMED!

TRANSFORMATION

...but be ye transformed
by the renewing of your mind,...
Romans 12:2 (KJV)

Transform my mind / Tired of the bind / Hung up in the old way / Time for a new day / Stuck on stuff that's inane / Continuing habits that are insane / Not growing in vision / Making the wrong decision / Trusting in my skill / Not heeding Your will / Leaning to my own choice / Oblivious to a higher voice / Really does not make sense / Self-centeredness is why I am tense / Must seek another direction / Listen to divine projection / All things start with You / A present help that's really true / Transforms what I am about / Let your grace be my lookout / Keep my eye on the goal / Renovation for my soul / No more resistance / Just follow Your insistence / Put aside my scheme / It's Your power that can redeem / Transform my mind / No comfort in being blind / Better to be ahead and not behind / Walk with me as I travel / Hold me when plans unravel / Restrain any self-pity / I seek a new city / Transform my mind / Let Your light shine / Keep me from leaning on what I think / Pride will make me sink / Can't get wisdom through pot and crack / That's really the wrong track / No more doing the strange / All about the change / Life is my occasion / Can be shaped by the right persuasion / Transform my mind / Discovering ways to be kind / That's a real find / Unearth my potential / Focused on the consequential / Being consistent in pursuit / Digging deep for the root / Guide me to a new destination / Enrich me with your revelation / Let me be Your new creation / Following You without hesitation / Changed to better material / Converting the natural to the spiritual / Transformed to do a new thing / A life lifted and taking wing /

IF YOU DEAL WITH THE WORLD WITHIN,
YOU CAN HANDLE THE WORLD WITHOUT.

WHO SAID NO?

...Hope thou in God: for I shall yet praise him, who is the health of my countenance, and my God
Psalm 42:11 (KJV)

Who said no? / They don't know what I know / I can grow and go / Keep my vision in tow / Can't get hung up on doubt/ My destiny is from the inside out / If I don't sit around whining / Can bring to life my own designing / Doesn't matter what others think / Fear and anxiety are weights that sink / I am God's child / Got the phone and can dial / No hang ups or busy sounds / God is available during His rounds / It's a done deal / Can't be stopped in His will / Keep the faith and don't falter / No challenge that God can't alter / Never mind what it may seem / The Master is real and heads my team / All things work for good / Got it goin' on with God in the hood / It's all about the right belief / Convinced that Heaven has relief / Why should I throw up my hand / God has promised to heal the land / Who said that life was not alive / They are fooled by their own jive / I got what I need / Get out of my way and let God lead / I found out it's for me if I just read / His Word is the seed / Tells me just to press toward the mark / God can light the dark / Let your faith stay alert / Don't be inert / Just exert / It's all up in here / Know whom to revere / And you will come out ahead in the game / Because you know

God is His name / Who said no? / Can't listen / It's time to go /

THERE'S NO STOPPING ME NOW!
READY OR NOT, HERE I COME!

WHERE ARE WE GOING?

When thou passest through the waters,
I will be with thee; ... when thou walkest through the fire, thou shalt not be burned...
Isaiah 43:2 (KJV)

Where are we going / Which way are we rowing / Seems like it's upstream / Still working on the dream / Got to fight the waves / Speaking peace makes them behave / "Peace be still" is the Lord's thrust / Don't falter and lose trust / It's a done deal / Triumph is in the Master's will / All will end up whole / God has the lead role / Offers us nurture and food / Shelter when it's rough and rude / Comfort in His sight / Guidance through the night / Full of hope for the day / God's prompt without delay / No matter how hard the test / It's true God leads the rest / No hesitation about destination / Ready to leave the station / Did our meditation / Have no angst or reservation / God's approved the pure and true / Ingredients for the Master's crew / It's about going in His name / He knows the rules of the game / They that look to achieve / Got to know who to believe / We can get ahead / God's alive and not dead / No value in laying back / Don't retreat - step up the attack / Go forward with drive / Stay up / Don't take a dive / Don't bow in the heat / We can compete / Hold steady on course / God is the real force / It's His power we tap / He's real and more than rap / Whatever comes down the river / God is the best giver / He looks out for our health / Lets us live on His wealth / Keep our head high / We shall live and not die / Victory is our mark / In times dark and stark / We're going ahead / Not lingering in bed / It's not a hard call / He'll never let us fall /

GOD'S GOT OUR BACK! STAY ON TRACK!

WHY WE ALWAYS CUSSING

Should a wise man utter vain knowledge....
Should he reason with unprofitable talk?...
Job 15:2-3 (KJV)

Tell me what's up with profanity / Just a form of verbal insanity / Using language that's vile / That makes the devil smile / Need to develop new talk. / Get ourselves another walk / Spewing out invective / Find ourselves a new directive / Shame on the stuff we say / Betraying fitness for a new day / Must really communicate / Time to orchestrate / Stop the swearing / Let's show some caring / Respect our community / Cussing shows mind disunity / No merit in talking foul / Wise up like the owl / Use our minds to draft liberation / Not containers for degeneration / Need a mental review / Dignity checkup is due / Learn how to embrace / Stop the speech of disgrace / Mothers are ashamed / Using our tongues to hurt and defame / Better to lift and kiss / More healthy than to diss and hiss / Time to do ourselves some good / Get the filth out of the hood / Young minds won't be polluted / Dreams soiled and hopes refuted / Give our future a chance / Speak of love and romance / Need to stop word crime / Right talk is on time / No more speaking nasty stuff / Not thinking – rapping off the cuff / Speech has power to hurt / Why deal in dirt / And with dumbness flirt / Tell you we must check our dialogue / Got to get out of this fog / Blow away the mist / Police our words – cease and desist / Better for all if talk doesn't scald / Cussing is wrong and small /

THE USE OF PROFANITY INDICATES A DEFICIT IN XPRESSION. IS YOUR CONVERSATION IN THE PLUS COLUMN?

WHY WE STILL FIGHTING?

What causes fights and quarrels among you? ...you quarrel and fight. You do not have because you do not ask God.
James 4:1-2 (NIV)

Why we still fighting / Putting down and slighting / Suffering wounds ain't charming / That's acting like hate's not harming / Killing is crazy - that's no doubt / Must put ignorance to rout / What a blessing in knowing / Cultivation and harmony keep seeds growing / It's a shame to hurt and pain / Loving others ought be our gain / What's the benefit in using a gun / No salvation when day is done / All the stuff we rob and steal / Don't mean nothing outside the Master's will / Time to stop packing / Ignorance is what we ought be attacking / Got to stop the folly / Pain and loss never makes you jolly / Hope that we get the news / It's our lives that we misuse / What's up with that / Ought to find a way to chat / Learn what real respect is about / Know it's more than hand signs and a shout / What up, dude? / Can't be up when habits got no glow / Living on the "down low" / Truth must be told / Dignity doesn't reside in cars and gold / Success is not what we wear / It's being real and meeting the dare / Speak a different word / Make love an "action verb" / Peace on earth ain't just for Christmas cards / It can blossom in our yards / Just need to stop buying the scam / Being aware will beat the sham / Honor is what we earn / Playing "hip" is the wrong turn / If we look within / Loving and living won't be just "every now and then" / We'll have some structure and order / Won't let dumbness cause disorder / Must sound the charge / Embrace the future and live large / It won't be hard to do / Reach for God / He's waiting for you /

FIGHTING INDICATES OUR FISTS ARE IN ACTION, BUT OUR MINDS ARE IN TRACTION.

WHY YOU ACT LIKE THAT?

[Love] doth not behave itself unseemly, seeketh not her own, is not easily provoked, thinketh no evil;
I Corinthians 13:5 (KJV)

Why you treat others like that / Crude and rude with no tact / Why you always talking loud / Looking to draw the crowd / Not in all that pretense / Your game is too intense / Why you act like that / Just offer the lonely an ear / Better than looking for a cheer / People deserve warmth and kindness / Self pride is coldness and blindness / Why you act like that / God wants us to be our brother's keeper / Aiding others is much deeper / More to life than mine / Also about "what's thine" / Better to put others first / Vanity just makes it worse / Need for compassion and care / What a blessing it is to share / Stop the putting down / Going around with a scowl and frown / Worried somebody wants to do you / Your fantasy just ain't true / God set us to make things brighter / Chase darkness and make spirits lighter / Fulfill your place on this earth / Accept the New Birth / Find out what happiness is worth / Let God give you direction / Don't be guilty of wrong affection / Won't have to ask the query / End the worry / A new choice is here / All who claim it erase gloom and fear / No more confrontation and agitation / End of vexation and frustration / What a change / Pride and vanity seem so strange / Indeed things are better / You can handle any weather / Why you act like that / Found out life is sweeter without tit for tat / Let it flow in God's stream / Life's richer than the dream /

LOOK IN THE MIRROR. DO YOU LIKE WHAT YOU SEE?

BE COOL

Thou wilt keep him in perfect peace, whose mind is stayed on thee:...
Isaiah 26:3 (KJV)

No need to worry / Why get in a hurry / God's still the boss / Can cope with every turn and toss / So just be cool / Don't act the fool / He won't ignore / Always stands at the door / Stop your fretting / He's not about forgetting / Believe He has your back / Provides where there's lack / The Lord never fails / Ears are open to our wails / So be cool / Stay under His rule / It's going to be alright / He's got the light / Trust your life with Him / Hangs with us when time seems dim / He holds us close / He masters without a boast / His love rates a toast / Covers us from coast to coast / Just got to stay calm / He's Gilead's balm / His record is great / On time and never late / Knows that all is well / Hell is not our jail / Be cool and stay, strong / He's there all day long / Guaranteed to deliver / He's with us at the river / Bears us through the tide / The Lord will provide / No need to sweat / The Master is the sure bet / Underneath are His arms / Our resource through the storms / Only trust His power / Watches us every hour / Can handle life's dare / Safe in His care / What a joy we share / He's there whether dark or fair / We have a winning deal / Secure in God's will / Like the poet's verse / God is there when it looks worse / Just secure in knowing /

His truth is still glowing / We have this peace / His essence is release / So be cool, be cool / No failure in God's school / Be cool. /

BEING COOL IS NOT OUTSIDE APPEARANCE BUT INSIDE TRUTH.

YOU ARE NOT ALONE

And yet if I judge, my judgment is true: for I am not alone, but I and the father that sent me.
John 8:16 (KJV)

Came to tell you when trials test your mettle / God knows how to settle / You are not alone / Be sure He is the cornerstone / Just keep your head up / He promises to help when problems disrupt / Trust that He will never fail / Never have to weep and wail / The Man is all you need / Got your back if you just heed / His love is there for you / Solve your worry and see you through / All your days are not sunny / Life is screaming and nothing's funny / Still you can laugh and smile / God helps you run your mile / Never put yourself down / Don't frown and blow your crown / It may be rough going / Take your faith and keep growing / Tests come to check your grit / Whether you march or just sit / The Master has a plan for you / A design that's sure and true / He won't leave you in a bind / Stumbling like the lost and blind / His vision charts the course / You can make it with soul force / Your comfort is in His power / Trust and don't cower / Listen to the peace in His voice / Evidence that it's the right choice / Real victory is in His care / His love is yours to share / Be happy that God is not dead / He supplies daily bread / He is right on time / His help is really prime / God's the truth and light / Leads through darkness and plight / He's on cue / To His word be true/ God just wants your belief / Recipe for your relief / It's really a cinch / It's God in the pinch / Whatever may come your way / God can keep it at bay / When all seems gone / God's here – you aren't alone /

GOD'S EYE CAN SEE MORE THAN YOU CAN SEE.
BE GLAD THAT HE IS WATCHING!

TIME FOR A CHANGE (1)

And that, knowing the time, that now it is high time to awake out of sleep:...
Romans 13:11 (KJV)

I am on a tread mill / I don't exercise my will / Do a lot of second guessing / Guilty of serious messing / Keep doing things that cause guilt / Practicing what makes me wilt / Rationalizing my mistake / Must change for truth's sake / Complaining has no virtue / Unwise to give it nurture / Decision to be is up to me / Only path to dignity / Time to stop lamenting / Better to start fermenting / No solution in hand wringing / Self-pity is stinging / Resolution is more than intent / Determination is the true content / Challenge is to stay on point / Trust Christ to anoint / Stop my wrong approach / Turn to the Cosmic Coach / End my inconsistency / Focus with real persistency / Christ conduct is rule of thumb / Anything else is just dumb / Affirming His example / His guidance is ample / It's my life to improve / Doing what Jesus would approve / Spinning my wheels is not winning / It's a deeper rut for sinning / Tired of "not taking a stand" / Equivocation won't take the land / Better to find peace of mind / Leave my excuses behind / It's the hour of decision / Give heed to the power vision / Look to God for aid / The debt has been paid / His love is real / Helps me up the hill / Just have to keep seeking / Prevent faith from leaking / Confronting my lack / It's folly to get off track / Can't afford to get derailed / Refuse to hear "I've failed" / Christ is still on the case / His will is the right taste / Must begin a life change / Give Him full range / Truth be told / My game is getting old / It's now or never / Time to pull the change lever /

**TIME DOESN'T STAND STILL.
DON'T LOOK AT ITS BACK.**

TIME FOR A CHANGE (2)

And he said: "Truly I tell you, unless you change and become like little children, you will never enter the kingdom of heaven.
Matthew 18:3 (NIV)

Time for a change / That's not strange / Time to go another way / Brighten the day / Don't delay / Try a different direction / Seek His protection / Life needs your skill / Guided by the Master's will / Doing nothing causes shame / Must respond or share the blame / There's a job that awaits / Do what God designates / Put your life in his hands / Obey His commands / God won't trick and slick / Take comfort as his pick / Just do what God says / He's your refuge for all days / Better to obey His teaching / Trust Him and keep reaching / Freed from our view/ God's plan is stronger than gorilla glue / Time to go from darkness to light / Forsake blindness for better sight / Time to believe that we can / Secure in the Lord's hand / Time to put down dope / Awake and seize hope / Time to reach within / Doing nothing will offend / Time to improve our condition / Escape from hell and perdition / God is where it's at / Always ready to go to bat / God's love never fails / Delivers us from vanity's jails / It's not the end of the rope / Lift our heads and cope / The answer is before us / God deserves our trust / If we're tired of the old game / Living what's lame and same / Give it to the Lord of life / End ignorance and strife / We carry a foolish load / Crazy to stay on a dead-end road / It's time for a change / God can arrange / No need to lose / God is the path to choose / Life need not estrange / Believe God / It's time for a change /

DINOSAURS DIDN'T CHANGE.
HAVE YOU SEEN ANY LATELY?

SINKING: WHY WE DOING THIS

Be not wise in thine own eyes: fear the Lord, and depart from evil.
Proverbs 3:7 (KJV)

Why are we doing this / Is it something I missed / Why are we raising hell / Keeping our minds in some crazy jail / What's the profit in strife / Violence fractures life / But we keep on hurting each other / Wounding dreams and ignoring mother / Children were brought here in pain / Destroying hope is no gain / Why we doing this / What's in it with such a risk / Need to wake up and think / Drugs and guns will make us sink / Wrong notion about success / Ought not to be based on some mess / Should be a source of pride / Give one another a ride / Yet we insist on gaming / Hurting others while cursing and blaming / Guess we have something loose / Not wise to fit our community for a noose / But we keep on doing wrong stuff / Blowing up dreams makes it tough / Only wish we would stop and think / Better to link than to sink / Why we doing this / Guess it's time for a new vision / Somebody got to make the decision / Must risk the danger / And brave the anger / Can't keep watching hope mangled / Victims of minds all tangled / Got to raise the issue for resolution / Get rid of the mental pollution / Will never get it right / Long as we don't strive for light / First thing is start resistance / Stay focused and be consistent / Wake up from deadly bliss / Ask ourselves - Why are we doing this /

CONFRONTATION IS THE WRONG WAY TO OUR DESTINATION.

WE SHOULD KNOW BETTER

There is a way which seemeth right unto a man, but the end thereof are the ways of death.
Proverbs 14:12 (KJV)

Killing the dream is a foolish act / No depth and lack of tact / All about sterility / An embrace of futility / Don't know why we choose to die / Messing up with a *drive by* / Still wondering what's the matter / Losing our vision in silly chatter / Ought to know better / Hanging out is not cool / Just a game with no school/ Minds gone to pot / Truth's seeds allowed to rot / Worry about things that mold / Sad result of a story not told / Been trying to offer a new way / Fruit of hope for this day / Life is worth more than money / Root of that which ain't funny / Worried about wealth we can't keep / Ought to trust and make the leap/ Never put your belief on cheap / Weighted down and can't reap / Keep going toward the dawn / Your life and values to spawn / Believe that you can rise to the task / Yours is victory if you just ask / It's the best approach / You can master with Jesus as coach / God is in charge / A truth rich and large / Stop your worry / Don't get in a hurry / Reap the joy of knowing / God is One who does the growing / About having more drive / Reaching the summit to survive / Knowing all things come to those who wait / Learn patience and how to relate / For Love won't cast you out / Still can laugh and shout / Discovered the reason why / Some don't get it and needlessly die / But if we learn our role / God has joy in us reaching the goal / Really got the Word on living / It's God who does the giving / And we can read the letter / Love of God is how we do better /

IT'S TIME TO LEAVE THE MINOR LEAGUE.
MAJOR LEAGUE BALL IS WHERE THE ACTION IS....

IN THE MIX WITH GOD

See then that ye walk circumspectly, not as fools, but as wise,

Ephesians 5:15 (KJV)

This is your day / Make it pay / You must score / Not less - but more / Opportunity is at your disposal / What's your proposal / Time is in your hand / Govern it by your command / Use it to bring change / Expand your influence and range / No virtue in laying back / Put your mind on track / Missing the boat is sad / Regret is a "feel bad" / So don't walk that trail / You must succeed - not fail / You are a super star in the making / Seize life - yours for the taking / All about your drive / Excel - not just survive / Why settle for less / God encourages being best / You won't flunk the test / Living in the positive mode / That's the believer's code / Looking to the bright side / No reason to hide / Help comes to the doer / No insight is truer / Get on with your scheme / Put some flesh on the dream / Stay with your vision / Commitment is the wise decision / Hesitation is not your game / Equivocating is big shame / You must sing your song / Don't mute it - do it strong / Your chance to advance / Avoid the loser's trance / Have to be alert / Sloth is a silly flirt / Blessings flow from the Lord / Give him reverence and regard / Offer Him thanks for your favor / Gratitude is a fine flavor / Acknowledge that you are touched by grace / Stamina to win the race /

All things work for your glory / God's love is a great story / Brought you from the bottom to the top / You are a winner - no flop / All praise to God / He gives you a wink and a nod / His attention is the "bomb" / Ignoring him is dumb / Be glad as you start your trek / God keeps the enemy in check / Your calling is to ascend / God's reliable - on that you can depend /

GOD IN THE MIX, WILL GET YOU OUT OF A FIX!

WAKE UP

... Awake thou that sleepest, and arise from the dead, and Christ shall give thee light.
Ephesians 5:14 (KJV)

Been sleeping too long / Time to get up and do it strong / Hanging out in the bedroom / No way to get to the boardroom / Wise up and alter our act / Change our mind - that's a fact / Can't lie around and talk / Secret is to rise and walk / Waking up is what we got to do / Reassess and do a new view / We conspire in our defeat / Staying in bed can only deplete / Time to hit the street / More to life than the bedroom suite / Need to take a new direction / Draft a game plan with deep reflection / Stop snoring / Do some exploring / Learn values that teach respect / Doing truth will have an effect / Time to wake up / Got to drink the cup / Handle what's on the plate / Get it done and don't be late / Nobody promised us an easy time / Feeling we can't is mind grime / We can find the road / Just need another mode / Wipe the sleep from our eyes / A winning strategy is what's wise / No reason to stay back / God's with us and that's no lack / Decide we want to do better / Write the world a letter / Tell the skeptics we are new creatures / Self-determination is among the best features / Critics won't find us in bed / Doing God's thing will get us ahead / Surprise those who said never / We discovered a new lever / And that's real clever / Ain't going to nap / Got the right map / It's about God and us / Right recipe for trust / Need to wake up / He promised He'd come in and sup / Time to wake up / Open our eyes wide / We can master the tide / God's by our side /

GET OUT OF THAT BED. DON'T PLAY DEAD!

BE A BELIEVER!

WISH I COULD

I must work the works of him that sent me, while it is day...
John 9:4 (KJV)

Wish I could do better / Really sit down and write the letter / Stop putting plans on the back burner / That's the sign of a slow learner / Must really do more than intend / Better method is to contend / Know that things need attention / Hell's road is paved with intention / Wish I could do more than sit and talk / Wish I could get up and walk / Wish I could make the day brighter/ Find a way to make the load lighter / Take some of the grief away/ Help others to know death ain't got to stay / Wish I could get others to see / Answers come in learning history / Can't keep on making the same error / Lost in ignorance is real terror / Wish I could pour some sense in others' heads / Secrets don't come from hanging in beds / Feel the urge to shout from the roof / Got to really stop being aloof / Wish I could get others to know / Love for people is the way to go / Wish I could do my teaching / Keep people seeking and reaching / Wish I could do more than wish / Poles out of water don't catch fish / Guess the beam is in my eye / Answer comes when I try / Wasting all this wishing is real crime / Should have been building with lost time / Glad I saw what was the block / It was my mind that was locked / Answers need more than wishing / Must hold fast when trouble is dishing / I really was confused / My talents I misused / Glad that the curtain was pulled back / Can overcome with my thoughts on track /

YOU CAN GO FROM WISHING TO WORKING

YES, WE CAN

The Lord is my light and my Salvation, whom shall I fear?...
Psalm 27:1 (KJV)

It's time to take a stand / It's in our hand / God supplies what we need / But it's His Word we must heed / Stop leaning to our own design / It's really about Divine Mind / Lets move to a new level / Don't get hung up on the devil / The real power is in the Masters will / His direction will give us zeal / We can do this thing / Just let our faith take wing / God is the power in this hour / Doing it alone is building a Babel tower / Not about us but God / Forgetting who's in charge is crazy and odd / Time for a new vision to speak / It's His truth that we must seek / It's all about believing in the Masters plan / Must follow His way and seize the land / It's really not hard to do / Just take the God view / Be certain of this fact / Victory will come as we act / God never fails / Our belief will ring victory bells / So rise up and do it / The formula is not where we sit / It's going in the Master's name / Any other will be of short fame / Our charge is to be open to the call / Inherit the wealth and stand tall / Yes we can / Yes we can! / Reach for the Master's hand / All things work out if we don't cop out / God surely wants us to succeed /And trusting Him is victory indeed /

YOU ARE LIMITED ONLY BY THE CEILING OF YOUR IMAGINATION.

GIVE IT TO HIM

And he arose, and came to his father. But when he was yet a great way off, his father saw him, and had compassion, and ran, and fell on his neck, and kissed him.
Luke 15:20 (KJV)

Talking about a real hero / Authentic man kind and no zero / The stuff of truth / He's also one hundred proof / Strong as a leader / Powerful provider and mouth feeder / Image in the home / Right there and won't roam / Hip as the rapper / It's his values that are dapper / Does not mess up the money / Knows his wife is the real honey / It's about more than sex / Sees life as more complex / Is an image for his offspring / A loving parent better than bling / Keeps his head on straight / Always able to relate / Father's Day is his due / Deserves that for being true / Give him all the gifts / His wisdom heals family rifts / He's our proud black king / Not phony but the real thing / Glad we are blessed through him / Vision giver when things get dim / So strike up the band / Father is the leading man / Tell you this without fear / Dad is the coolest dude here / Salute those who have a father's name / Also live up to the claim / This is your day of praise / Honor is yours with voices raised / We stand in celebration / Father is worthy of commendation / This is your day to chill / We honor you and that's a thrill / So men of worth / You really are of noble birth

/ God has something in you / Keep on living to the higher view / Happy Father's Day / Stay strong on the way / Keep your principles in line / You are vineyard and wine / This is your day / May you prosper and stay / This is your day / That's what we say / That's what we say / Yea, Yea, Yea / To Fathers / Hooray, Hooray! /

THIS IS WHAT A HERO IS ABOUT.
I DON'T CARE WHAT HOLLYWOOD SAYS

A FATHER'S PLACE

Train up a child in the way he should go: and when he is old, he will not depart from it.
Proverbs 22:6 (KJV)

Father in the room / Chaser of fear and gloom / A presence that offers cheer / Joy trumpeting when he's near / Never leaves his children alone / Has earned his place on the throne / Positioned by their bed / He's a very secure head / A wisdom that guides / Duty which provides / Protection for their way / Available without delay / Father's place is where the children play / He's near day-to-day / A father's place has no space / Just stay on pace / Goes wherever children run / Vigilance shielding to the setting sun / Father's place is at school / Their mind is a precious tool / Challenging them to study well / Always responding to learning's bell/ Encouraging to make wise choices / Listening to the right voices / Informing them to master the text / Counsel when it's complex / A father's place is never zoned / As close as the cell phone / Stands ready to rescue/ Conscious of any venue / Father's place is spirit connection / It's a bond of deep affection / Transcends the easy description / Always got the right prescription / Watches through every test / Promoter of the best/ Father's place has no restriction / His love is a benediction / More than an absent father stereotype /

Real fathers beat the hype / Fulfills the ideal / Parent accepting God's will/ Not hung up on ego / Open to God's flow / Father's place is by their side / Constant despite the tide / Whether it whips a strong foam / He's present wherever they roam / A father's place is not here or there / It's truly everywhere / Wherever the children skip and shout / That's father's place - no doubt / So on this Father's Day we boast / Real fathers deserve a toast / It's more than Mother's duty / Father love has truth's beauty / Light up the time / Praise father with a ringing chime / Men can fill the role / Child caring is a worthy goal / I just want to use this space / Give a shout-out to a father's place.

LIFE IS MORE THAN I TOLD YOU SO.
IT'S GIVING OTHERS A CHANCE TO GROW.

MOTHERLESS CHILD

Come, ye children, hearken unto me: I will teach you the fear of the Lord.
Psalm 34:11 (KJV)

Sought for some help on the road / Told I had to bear the load / Momma died the other day / Left me in a rough way / Talking about momma you see / Never saw the man called daddy / Anyhow got to keep my stride / Can't get mad if there's no free ride / I know what momma taught / Don't sell out or let your pride be bought / I am a creature of worth / Have been special since my birth / Ignore the critics' view / Keep telling myself to be true / Keep seeking my goal / Just be faithful and let it unfold / There's no salve in self-pity / Only mastery will take the city / What mother gave was respect / Value system that won't defect / A belief that defeat is my fault/ Giving in when I need to vault / Mother is still urging me to be straight / Don't bend and accept my fate / Whining is excuse for the weak / But there's more if I choose to seek / Can't forget lessons at momma's knee / Undaunted faith - that's the key / Hang in and keep driving / I'm responsible to keep thriving / Momma left me a code to follow / Without honor - success is hollow / Told me conviction can cope / Never sell my dreams to dope / That's putting my neck in a rope / Momma's "presence" is my support / She's daily checking the report / Her counsel is not in the physical / Yet she's real beyond the mystical / I may be a child whose mother is gone / But really, I'm not alone / Mother's teachings are still my guide / Her spirit says: the Lord will provide /

BETTER BE GOOD! MOTHER'S GOT HER EYES ON YOU!

THE SUNDAY PARADE

When he came near the place where the road goes down the Mount of Olives, the whole crowd of disciples began joyfully to praise God in loud voices...
Luke 19:37 (NIV)

The Jesus tour was in town/ Some wore a frown / They came to watch the show / Minds in the wrong flow / Jesus came to make it plain / New life is on the freedom train / Vision time will spread / Courage in crisis drives ahead / Got to take the ride / Promise is that God will provide / Can't dodge destiny's call / Truth will rise and not fall / Time to robe up like God's son / Staying strong till the course is run / The focus must be on the goal / Struggle was always about man's soul / A faith confronting the harsh assault/ Grace sufficient for vanity's fault / The crowd was dumb to the time / Surely that is the cutting crime / They could have gone to sublime heights / It's a fool's choice to wander in ignorant nights / Jesus observed the whole drama / That day was a pitiful panorama / People were talking what they did not know / Spreading dead seeds that could not grow / He rode on with flint-like resolve / A commitment that "crucify him" would not dissolve / The shouts of hosanna rang loud / He felt a sadness for the parade crowd / For all the buzz and heavy praise / Jesus accepted these moments as end days / Look how they call his name / A clamor that will soon be thoughtless shame / Jesus found a garden to reflect / It was the fullness taking effect / He thought as tears mixed with a sigh / It was really his mission to die / Let the parade march its way / Jesus did not come to stay / He who served in the Lord's name / It's Friday's act that wins the game.

YOU MAY MARCH IN THE PROCESSION.
IT'S TIME OUT FOR DIGRESSION.

RESURRECTION

...I am the resurrection, and the life ... and whosoever liveth and believeth in me shall never die....
John 11:25-26 (KJV)

The gathering clouds shadow the day. The sun seems to have taken a sabbatical. But the teaching of your example is that darkness shall not reign on the throne. It is our assurance that Your power for deliverance is undiminished. It is in You that we discover incentives for insightful and indomitable living. We offer gratitude for the prestigious potency of the resurrection. The continuing impact of the triumph over death and dislocation energizes our hopes and galvanizes our momentum. Death does not have the last word. Your conquest of death's dire designs empowers us to stand tall in the saddle of service.

There is no way that our belief cannot but be enhanced as we rehearse the majesty of your triumph. Chaos does yield to Cosmos. Peace soothes the anguished spirit. Deliverance has the skeleton key for our release. Resurrection has not folded its witness like a seasonal garment only to be worn at the formal ball celebrating the Easter experience. It is, however, a vibrant continuation which guides our faith walk.

The intimacy and immediacy of the resurrection keeps our spiritual engines revved for the ongoing journey. We are equipped to contend against the principalities and powers.

There is rejuvenation in knowing that we are not alone. It is your personal promise that you will be with us throughout time. Such joyous conviction offers optimism for eternity's drama. We are ready to move to the next level of spiritual uniqueness.

Speak to our expectations with the mastery of your majesty. There is no venue for fear and futility. We are confident that the resurrection reality will indeed keep us saturated in satisfaction. We have a comfort too strong to be defeated or depleted by emergencies or unexpected crises.

The continuity of the resurrection experience is our insurance that our claims will be covered. We are protected from error with empathy and from despair with the knowledge that you are our hope.

YOU CAN GET UP OUT OF THE BED.
BEDS ARE FOR SLEEPING. LIFE IS FOR REAPING

HEAVEN IN VIEW

But Stephen, full of the Holy Spirit, looked up to heaven and saw the glory of God, and Jesus standing at the right hand of God.
Acts 7:55 (NIV)

I got some place to go / Where flowers bloom and dreams grow / It's an estate of many riches / Worth all the glitches and hitches / It's a place where things never grow old / A land where there's a story to be told / It drives me on to live in that home / No more need to search and roam / It's all about new joy / True happiness free from alloy / Heaven's a cool place / The victor's prize after the race / Can kick back and chill out / Going to see the glory and what it's about / Don't have to worry about drive-bys and disrespect / It's about stop-bys and love's project / Where we greet in holy mirth / Experience the reward of the new birth / Plan to take a tour of heaven's sights / It's a good thing filled with delights / It's going to be some shouting when I get there / All celebrating because Jesus did care / Believe it / I'm going to really have a divine ball / Plenty of fun for obeying the Master's call / So look out / All those who arrived before me / Strike up the band / It's my time for gaiety / Indeed, it's all about knowing what to do / Heaven is the universe of God's crew / Going to step up and join the team / At last, I have realized my dream /

HEAVEN IS THE BEST ALTERNATIVE TO HELL!

IT'S MORNING TIME

It is of the Lord's mercies that we are not consumed because his compassions fail not. They are new every morning:...
Lamentations 3:22 (KJV)

The day spreads its arms / Invitation to its many charms / It's morning time/ Choices are sublime / It's our call / Rise or fall / Excuse making is so wrong / No way to live it strong / We can change the game / Stop acting lame / Put on a new face / Get in the race / All we need is conviction / That's a real benediction / Doors are not locked / Roads aren't blocked / Must get on up / Drink from morning's cup / Plenty of things to do / Focus on the right view / No virtue in fear / Opportunity is here / All about our belief / That's how we spell relief / It's not an over-the-counter pill / It's the size of our will / We must choose to use / Can't act confused / Up to us to move / Find the power groove / Make the day come alive / Give it a high five / No option in taking a dive / That's crazy and won't survive / God is not dead / Trust Him to get ahead / Put faith in His way / Recipe for a great day / Seek divine direction / Embrace His affection / Stay close to God / There's strength in His rod / Will always supply our need / That's why we avoid greed / There's unlimited supply / Keep God nearby / The morning is upon us / In God we trust / It's our decision / The Lord is provision / No need for revision / Just follow His scheme / We claim the dream / Morning time is where we start / Plan the journey's chart / Give it our heart / Let God take part / We have success without fail / He's the head – never the tail / There's comfort in His Word / Our cry is surely heard / Reason we embrace the day / Help is on the way / Be still and know / Life is ours to grow / Listen to His command / Occupy and take the land / Morning arrives with a shout / God is what it's about / We are going to cross the line / God with us is fine / He is more than we can utter / The morning has opened its shutter /

TODAY IS OUR GIFT FROM GOD

DAYLIGHT SAVING TIME

...For it is time to seek the Lord, until he comes and showers his righteousness on you
Hosea 10:12 (NIV)

We have an extra hour / Make it sweet - not sour / Time is a blessing / Use it for day dressing / That's a name for wise use / Acting soberly - not loose / Got an extra hour / Sit around or build a tower / Need to not waste the bonus / Ignorant use would be an onus / Hope we act with sense / Erase what keeps us tense / We prance around like royalty / Need to have some loyalty / Put the saving to wise employ / Dispense some love and joy / This daylight cheats the dark / Need to do more than sit in the park / Working wisely hits the mark / It's serious, not a lark / Yeah, we got some time / Let's make life more sublime / Let life's bell ring and chime / Really must give an account / Did we lead others to the fount / Offer a drink of kindness / Defeat our thirst for blindness / Should really use this hour / Invest it with love power / More "doesn't" mean a thing / Wisdom's touch must take wing / Did we help the lost / Banish pride's high cost / It's about being humane / Being mean is the wrong vein / Must not harm / Bringing the death storm / Really need some charm / Fellowship should be the norm / This is just a thought / Lessons must be taught / Yeah, we got more time to see / What we gonna leave for posterity / Daylight saving time / Worth more than a nickel or dime / Right use stops the crime / Got some daylight / Raise our sight / Erase the blight / Light the night / So, we have this hour / Better use it / Time for peace to flower /

DON'T WASTE TIME. LIFE IS NOT A DRESS REHEARSAL.

CHANGE

...ye can discern the face of the sky; but can ye not discern the signs of the times?
Matthew 16:3 (KJV)

Television news shames us / All about the lack of trust / People dying in a violent manner / Killers waving a defiant banner / What sadness we share / Time to really care / Reports of deaths lose urgency / Just the price of insurgency / But it's really an emergency / Time to end the madness / No joy in this sadness / Why are we so tame / We wear the Jesus name / Ought to speak loud and clear / Can't be silenced by fear / Must not accept the "go along" rule / Can't just act like a dumb mule / We have minds to reason / And this is our due season / This hour is pressing / It's all about addressing / Closing our minds is a crime / This is a critical time / Called to the kingdom for this / Transforming foolishness into bliss / Stopping the maiming / That's worth claiming / Got to end sorrow / What will happen tomorrow / Can't keep twiddling our fingers / Ignorance yet lingers / When are we going to change / Must we end with a bang / This is really a mess / Are we doing our best / Those who do faith talk / Better pick up our walk / It's in the final stage / Man must stop the rage / We have a job to do / It's really whether we are false or true / No excuse for shuffling / Yes, some feathers need ruffling / This is a just cause / No reason to pause / Leaders must hear our rejection / Their policy is the wrong direction / Got to say it clear and loud / God is not proud! God is not proud!

YOU ARE CALLED TO BE A DIFFERENCE MAKER!

THIS IS THE DAY

But seek ye first the kingdom of God, and his righteousness; and all these things shall be added unto you.
Matthew 6:33 (KJV)

This is the day that God made / Don't give up and fade / Hold to the vision / The Lord makes provision / Focus on your dream / Not as tough as it seems / Can't throw in the towel / Build with a faith trowel / God's got all you need / Time to give heed / Keep your head high / Don't purchase a sigh / I know it's easy to feel sorry / Perplexed that the nights not starry / But God is alive / You can yet arrive / You are never without hope / You can handle the slope / Stay positive and cope / This is your hour / He's a mighty tower / You can bear the load / Rest stops on the road / God won't let you down / Get rid of that frown / Though there are tests and trials / Life still has smiles / God does care / He will share / Won't cast you aside / His love will preside / His strength is for you / His word is true / Failure is not His style / He'll answer your dial / Call Him on the prayer cell / He will answer the bell / God will aid / End the doubt raid / You can carry the load / Discover the faith code / Never say never / God's wisdom is clever / Success is on the way / Chasing shadows like a sun ray / Just keep looking up / Defeat can't disrupt / All things work for good / God's power says: that's understood / It's really a great day / God has the final say / That's shouting material / Glad that joy is spiritual / Going to do a praise song / It's always God that keeps you strong / Hallelujah! Life has satisfaction / God is still the main attraction. /

IT'S A GREAT DAY! IF YOU DON'T THINK SO, TRY MISSING ONE!!

PENTECOST

When the day of Pentecost came, they were all together in one place.
Acts 2:1 (NIV)

Disciples with mission goals / Spirits touched by flaming coals / Apostles on the go / Drenched with Holy Ghost glow / Sending a signal to the world / Faith's banner unfurled / Success for the church / Nobody left in the lurch / Dawn of a bright beginning / A formula for winning / Release from weakness / Power chasing bleakness / Holy Spirit on the case / Surely worth a taste / Power flowing from its core / Really is the way to soar / Going in the Spirit's name / New rules in the game / Anointing from sacred fire / The Church's aid from wire to wire / Holy Ghost is no sham / Envoy of the "Great I Am" / Sanctioned by the Savior / It's holiness in flavor / Assistance in preaching / Insight for teaching / Expanding its reaching / Pentecost running strong / Witnessing all the day long / Sent as a sign / A paradigm that's divine / Uplifting the worn and torn / An empowered church being born / Pentecost is a shining light / A church governed by spiritual sight / No walking in error / Sin loses its terror / Pentecost is the new creation / That's worth a celebration / Happy that the spirit is in charge / Chasing all sin at large / Now is

Pentecost Day / It came without delay / It's worth shouting and dancing / The Holy Spirit is the kingdom advancing /

**LIKE MINDS GENERATE POWER.
WATCH YOUR ASSOCIATIONS**

HE GOT UP

He is not here, but is risen:...
Luke 24:6 (KJV)

We thought the grave was His jail / it was over, He had failed / Had Him under lock and key / The tomb was our victory / Imagine the surprise and fear / Told by guards He's not here / What could this mean / His burial had been seen / Now there's no Jesus / His absence can't please us / He's up and gone / Somebody's moved the stone / What a mess on our hand / History will stir the land / Must cook up a fable / Pretend He wasn't able / Tell the world the grave was robbed / Taken away by a mob / What can we do / Can't admit he was true / He got up / Beat the cross and bitter cup / Exhibited power and zeal / Look how He broke the Roman seal / Guess He will live forever / Must admit He's mighty clever / Left some egg on our face / Fooled us - not in place / No matter how we planned / His truth can't be banned / Makes us angry as hell / A lie we must tell / Jesus beat us down / Really does wear the crown / Have to acknowledge / He knew more than any college / Now He's loose in the land / Wonder what's His plan / He's got us on our heels / Has shamed our lies and deals / Don't know how it came about / He's not there but got out / Guess we didn't know / He still had seeds to sow / His disciples will till the ground / Proof that his teachings are sound / Despite our scheme and plot / Three days and no body rot / Backed up what He said / Refused to stay dead / Doubters may trick and contend / One thing's for sure / He really did win /

YOU CAN'T KEEP A GOOD BELIEVER DOWN!

THE WAY

I am the way the truth, and the life
John 14:6 (KJV)

He's the path out of despair / A presence always there / An escape from the trap / His Word is the map / His trust has no fault / No reason to waffle and halt / He is the Way / Resource for our day / Reside in His skill / Christ can take the hill / He wants us to be still / Submit to His will / Stop getting in a hurry / A habit that is sure to worry / The wiser manner is reliance / Trust Him – stay in compliance / It's better to put God first / He can handle the worst / Must suppress our ego / Avoid unnecessary woe / Practice the plan / Reach for His hand / His way is not our style / Doesn't rest on wile and guile / Always embracing our progress / No way we should regress / His way is the best / Assurance in every test / The road to peace / Guarantor of sweet release / The avenue to mirth / Reward for the new birth / Comfort in His love / Available from push to shove / Gives us faith for a guide / He never fails to provide / He's the way beyond defeat / His strength is complete / Captures us in His arms / No reason for fear's alarms / His vigilance won't falter / Look at the Psalter / Better listen to his teaching / Take guidance from His beseeching / Pay attention to His code / Sin is a heavy load / Stay close by His side / Let His truth abide / Jesus knows how to lead / His wisdom fits every need / We just have to slow our roll / His acceptance is our goal / Just temper our new school "smarts" / His knowledge is off the charts / He will take us to a higher plane / Obedience is our gain / His triumph will not recede / Get out of the lane – let Him lead /

THE JESUS WAY WILL MAKE YOUR DAY!

EXPECT A MIRACLE

...for there is no man which shall do a miracle in my name that can lightly speak evil of me.
Mark 9:39 (KJV)

Hemmed up at the Red Sea / Pharaoh messing with our destiny / Got his troops on our trail / Planning to assault and assail / His chariots sound like thunder / An army to take us under / Trying to stop the flight / Keep us in fright and plight / Certain that he has the military / Mocking us as ordinary / Can't wait to stop our trek / Turn our march into a wreck / His plot is to lay waste / Destroy us with haste / Puffed up in his pride / Knowing we cannot hide / Rubbing his hands in anticipation / Glorying in our extermination / Already planning a victory celebration / Praising his might with exhilaration / But we have a Word from the Lord / His assurance is our sword / Just have to stretch out in hope / It's faith that can cope / Expect a miracle to unfold / Hold fast and be bold / Despite how the battle appears / God is worthy of our cheers / Tells us to focus on Him / Won't leave us out on the limb / Expect darkness to become light / Trust Him through faith's sight / Lift up our aspiration / God delivers from desperation / Whenever our challenges cause fret / God is the best yet / His help guards our rear / We can win over fear / Let Pharaoh be the example / God's deliverance is more than ample /Red

Seas come in various ways / God is still author of our days / When it looks grim / Turn to Him / When issues are chilling / God is ever willing / Despite the dead end / He promises to defend / Expect a miracle in the storm / God's overcoming is the norm / Holy Writ is our guide / Jehovah Jireh does provide / Stay tuned to His direction / Trusting triumphs over dejection / We are going through / His help is true / Expect the miracle for our blessing / With God there's no guessing / So when Pharaoh mounts the attack / God will push him back / Expect the miracle for our advance / Pharaoh never stood a chance /

GOD HAS A MIRACLE WITH YOUR NAME ON IT!

FINISH WHAT YOU STARTED

RUNNING

Holding forth the word of life; that I may rejoice in the day of Christ, that I have not run in vain, neither laboured in vain.
Philippians 2:16 (KJV)

I am on the run / Have a race that's not done / A challenge before me / Striving for the victory / Not running scared / Just grateful His love is shared/ It's my task to persist / No way that I resist / Called to the Kingdom to work / Not a time to shirk / Calling is about striving / A ministry of reviving / Goals to be accessed / No time for recess / Running with hope in my heart / Know it's all about a new start / Putting down old ways / Fitted for new days / Ready to stay the course / God is the source / The joy of completing / A maturity beyond competing / I am on the run / Rising before the sun / Sleeping is old school / My mind is a tool / Fitted to do the task / Can't wear the slothful mask / Realize it's an opportunity / Hope and desire in unity / Staying with the assignment / Avoiding mind confinement / Keeping my energy at the ready / Doing it sure and steady / There is overcoming in belief / Just know who is chief / God is the head / Wants me alive and not dead / Must run with insight / Darkness fades before light / So glad that I know / Running hard is how to grow / This is my hour / Hanging in whether sweet or sour / God is watching my face / Must never lose pace / Pressing toward the finish / His strength will replenish / Too close to go slow / Still some grass to mow / Proud that God is concerned / He cares about what I discern / That gives me greater zest / God with me is the best / It's the wind at my back / I really am on track / Going to shout and sing / God is the Real Thing / Only trust His power / I have a suite in the victory tower / I did do the run / Not all fun / But God sent his Son /

JESUS IS ALWAYS READY
FOR AN EARLY MORNING RUN. JOIN HIM!

STOP THE DOUBTING

(For we walk by faith, not by sight:)
II Corinthians 5:7 (KJV)

It's not my world that I made / When I see the sun rise and then day fade / Witness the majesty of the clouds play / See flowers blooming in every way / Ought to know that this place is no accident / Everything has order by divine providence / Since it was here when I got here / Really rates a cheer / Can't afford to act like I know what's it all about / Looking deep and profound as I doubt / I may have a few degrees and know a thing or two / But really don't know the secret if I am just being true / It's all a game to pretend my facts are the real story / I'm still stumped about the mystery of the *morning glory* / If there's rhythm to the flower time / Surely must admit wonder rings like a bell chime / Got to stop talking as if I know it all / I'm just an infant whose experience is small / Learning to walk involves some falling / Yet destiny speaks, "You have a calling" / You can stand on your own feet / Just know that the trip is yours to complete / Looks shaky and crazy at first / But the floor's hardness is not the worst / Release your fear and step to the prize / It's all about what's in your eyes / Even though trial and error can be a trip / It's helpful to take His tip / This world was designed for your life / Don't borrow from sorrow and make strife / Never doubt that your presence is part of the Master's plan / Know that you won't be an also ran / Go on and get what's yours / Faith still opens doors / My advice in starting out / Walk by faith and don't doubt. /

IF YOU DOUBT, YOU'LL BE SHUT OUT!
DON'T YOU WANT TO COME INSIDE?

BAGGAGE

Let us lay aside every weight, and the sin which doth so easily beset us,...
Hebrews 12:1 (KJV)

Traveling light is the way to go / Easier to get to and fro / No hassles at the gate / Inspection is what I hate / TSA rummaging in your bags / Checking down to name tags / Really can be a trip / Should take this tip / Leave the luggage at home / Better way to roam / Baggage is a real concern / Doesn't take long to discern / But it's not just the bags we check / There's baggage that's up to our neck / Bags that are not vinyl or leather / Bags that weigh more than a feather / We get heavy and slow / Baggage won't let us grow / Traveling from place to place / Baggage doesn't help the race / Baggage can weight us down / Make us frown / Can blow the crown / Baggage is a heavy load / No joy for the road / Need to strip away the excess / Retain what can pass the test / Crazy to carry what we don't need / Lesson we should heed / Should get rid of over packing / Practice which shows where we are lacking / Stuffing our luggage is a metaphor / Habit that says: no way to soar / If we want to fly / Light packing is worth a try / But this is about more than trains, boats and planes / It's about assessing losses and gains / Baggage makes travel a drag / Its heaviness makes spirits sag / Burdened with cares and worry / Enough to make our vision blurry / Slowed by fears and fright / Recipe for remaining uptight / Ignoring God who is able / A help that is stable / Just call for His aid. / The debt is already paid / No reason to be lurching / His love is always searching / Seeking to lift our heads / Ends the tossing on our beds / Provides a remedy for lost sleep / Gives rest that's deep / Now He has us in hand / Listen to His command / Be still and hear / Overweight travels in the wrong gear /

TRAVELING LIGHT HELPS WHEN THINGS GET TIGHT. GOD'S STILL AROUND IF WE HAVE TO SPEND AN OVERNIGHT.

IT'S MORE THAN TALK

All hard work brings a profit, but mere talk leads only to poverty.
Proverbs 14:23 (NIV)

All you do is talk / You must also walk / Just carrying lame conversation / No way to save the nation / Sitting around talking smack / Ain't going to earn even a snack / Better to put some legs on words / Empty talk is for the birds / Wish you would stop the chatter / Really see what's the matter / People who are always rapping / Need to spend some time mapping / Got to get some action / Talking too much puts our tongues in traction / Must back up what we say / Make plans for a new day / Chart a bold vision / Less talking is the right decision / The Word must become flesh / Stale chatting needs to be refreshed / Get done with verbalizing / Get some actualizing / Stop the preaching / Let's do some reaching / Leave the soap box / Be wise like the fox / Don't bark without reason / Draws attention in the hunting season / Know how to keep your mouth closed / Act like your voice froze / Keep them guessing about your plot / Loose lips reveal a lot / Put your mind to better use / Foolish talk makes a noose / Be still and look deep / Don't sell yourself cheap / Keep your thoughts like precious pearls / Be quiet when storms whirl / For it's clear without doubt / Silence is often the best way out/ So, let them guess about your view / Opening my mouth may be cause for rue / I really am convinced / Less talk makes more sense. /

STOP THE TALKING AND BEGIN WALKING!

WHY ARE WE STANDING HERE

...and they said one to another, Why sit we here until we die?

II Kings 7:3 (KJV)

It's time to go and get it done / Put doubt and confusion on the run / No sense in hanging in the cut / Got to get our mind out of the rut / We must not be our own block / Stop getting hung up on the clock / Let's be about heeding the Master's time / Doing it our way is spiritual crime / Only what God has instructed / That also is what must be constructed / Why are we standing here / What is there to fear / Faith has the ingredient of cheer / Never worry because God's love is near / No need to start and stop / We can make it to the top / Now, let's not stand in our light / Fretting about our plight / God removes worry and fright / All we have to do is go with faith and not sight / There's gold in them "thar hills" / Available to those who avoid the devil's deals / No treasure is enough to dissuade our task / We are not duped by the enemy's false mask / Our gain is already assured / God's love is available to those who have endured / No longer must we just hang around / It's the age of "getting our crown" / And we won't miss the celebration / God calls us to the true coronation / *Let the redeemed of the Lord say so* / We really have eternity seeds to sow / Our dreams shall be wrapped in His care / We discover God is pleased when we take the dare /

STANDING AROUND, JUST LEADS TO MORE STANDING AROUND. ARE YOUR FEET TIRED?

SO WHAT

Commit thy way unto the Lord; trust also in him; and he shall bring it to pass.
Psalm 37:5 (KJV)

Trouble may come to your door / You can still get off the floor / Trials and trauma may clutter your way / So what, it's still a good day / Things may tumble and rumble / Some good chances you may fumble / So what / No reason to start crying / That will keep you from trying / Life was not designed to make you feel good / Sometimes like being lost in a dark wood / So what / Each day is still a pearl / Just claim the oyster in your world / May not always be warm and rosy / Still got to do it when your zone is not cozy / So what if things become a little rough / You are more than fluff / Must go forward when the fog rolls in / God's servant must cope and still win / It's about what you desire / All yours if you keep the fire / So what if you don't get support / You have to believe the report / It's God who is in charge / Whatever happens – no issue is too large / So what if doubters turn the day gray / It's true the Lord will make a way / So hang in there / Stand up and take the dare / God won't leave you alone / Does not fall asleep on the throne / There is a path out of the trap / God will provide the map / So what if it seems that it's more mess and duress /

You can stand the test /And gain your success / It's really your heart that guarantees a fresh start / Employing faith makes the best life chart / So what if others criticize / It's in Him that your dreams are realized /

YOU MUST MASTER CIRCUMSTANCES.
NEVER ALLOW CIRCUMSTANCES
TO BE YOUR MASTER.

BELLING THE CAT

Is anything too hard for the Lord?...
Genesis 18:14 (KJV)

Cats are not friends of mice / View is they are not nice / Would be wise to hear their approach / Discovering a way beyond reproach / Mice minds came up with a plan / To take things in hand / Put a bell on the cat / That would settle that / Every mouse gave a roar/ Except one by the door / He raised his hand for order / Asked about the cat's border / Who would take the bell / Risk what could be hell / How would the bell be attached / Would require courage unmatched / To bell the cat is fine / Who's first in line / And then the silence fell like a veil / No takers of the bell / And that's a lesson for us / Talk without acting is dust / Belief must scale the hill / Fear freezes the will / The cause demands grit / Can't just sit / The issue is tough / Can't just act off the cuff / Realize the danger is real / Sacrifice demands courage and zeal / Are we willing to take a bold step / To go where success is kept / It's a prize for the brave / Can't dwell in doubt's cave / It takes more than a chat / Planning will bell the cat / Our cat is not just feline / Other things come to mind / Belling the cat is what we avoid / Not wanting to stay on guard / Can't get trapped in self-deception / Belling the cat is the right weapon / Demands that we defeat our fear / God has promised to be near / Despite the size of the test / God-partnering is best / The cat has sharp paws / Awareness avoids its jaws / We must know God never fails / Many cats wear His bells / We just go in His skill / Stay focused on His will / God likes to bell the cat / Trusting Him is where it's at / God does it through us / His way is true and just / The cat is just a symbol / God's grace is more nimble / God uses the cat to show / His grace is the brightest glow / If we sow seeds / God meets our needs / Just wants to demonstrate / He's on time and never late / Know that the cat ain't all that / Often bragging through its hat / Goliath was acting like he was bad / He too "got had" / Cats are just one of God's tools / Belling them are lessons in His schools / Offers us a chance to see / Belling cats is a faith strategy / Putting our fate in His power / Victory is not the cats – it's ours / Looks scary at first / But cat belling is not the worst / What's really the greatest error / Not trusting God to end the terror /

THE BELL IS IN YOUR HAND!

DON'T LET IT GET YOU DOWN

He will call upon me, and I will answer Him; I will be with him in trouble, I will deliver him and honor him
Psalm 91:15 (NIV)

Don't be bound – down to the ground / Things seem kind of rough / What you bit off is kind of tough / Feel like throwing up your hands / Seems like you lost command / Keep on working / Self-pity is lurking / Hang in with all you can / God is still head of the land / Tears may come rushing out / Yet the Lord knows what it's about / Burdened like a homeless child / Don't give up – God's got your file / Despite trials and setbacks / God provides grace comebacks / His love is not weak / Turn to Him when its bleak / His angels will hasten to aid / Got your back without being paid / Know that Satan ain't the last word / God is Omega, ain't you heard / All the schemes and plots / No way you gonna be tied in knots / Promise is fulfilled by God's reliance / Can't be beaten with his alliance / Don't let it sweat you – all of the mess / God is true in duress / Be still and stop wailing / No record of God failing / Just wait and don't hang your head / The Lord will lift it instead / You're going to succeed / Trust your Savior to feed and lead / I know that you can get down in the dumps / Yet, His love gets you over the humps / Never fear what's lying in the grass / God's victory will come to pass / What joy in your soul / You have scored the goal / Forget how the foe says no / God's seed is what you sow / And even though events may frown / Don't get down / You have a waiting crown. /

YOU ARE A JACK-IN-THE BOX! KEEP ON GETTING UP!

STUCK

...If God be for us, who can be against us?
Romans 8:31 (NIV)

Sometimes I am stuck / Mired in muck / Out of luck / Dodging that truck / Seems that fortune has fled / Laughed and left me for dead / Temptation to whine and moan / Figuring why I groan alone / Spending my hours in pity / Stranded in the city / But it's my call / Give up or scale the wall / Up to me to act / Find the contact / God's alive and that's a fact / Stop oiling my fear / That's a path that's severe / Time to put a new attitude in gear / Christ is near / His life is real / Trusting Him is a better deal / Releases me to explore / Got supplies in His store / Blessings for the seeker / Other choices make me weaker / Crazy not to accept / His love is not inept / Futility may weave its blame / Christ says trust His name / Stay on point / His spirit will anoint / Be open and receive / It's time to believe / Can choose to stay chained / Not heeding what's explained / Told me to observe / Helps me to hit life's curve / Steadies me in my going / Looking out for my growing / Christ is "real people" / Shout it from the valley to the steeple / Patience is waiting to receive / Confident he does not deceive / He will set me free / Sponsors my jubilee / Delivers me to higher height / Reveals His light / Heeding His sight / Not stuck in the night / Sweet breeze of peace / Trusting Him is my release / Glad that I broke from the pity cell / Christ chains my hell / It's worth a shout / Christ helps to work it out / No longer stuck / It's about faith and not luck. /

JESUS IS HANDS ON.
HE PUTS HIS LOVE INTO PRACTICE.

I'M GOING THROUGH

In this was manifested the love of God toward us, because that God sent his only begotten Son into the world, that we might live through him.

I John 4:9 (KJV)

Got my ticket in hand / Looking for the Promised Land / Left my home with haste / Had to enter the chase / God gave me the map / Couldn't just nap / Searching for a city / No handout for pity/ Empires come to those who build / Product of faith and will / Don't know the exact path / God and I are the right math / Can't fail with the mandate / Go forward and innovate / Marching to new heights / Bringing gardens from blight / Planting new seeds on the shore / Life leaping from belief's core / Can't be turned from my view / I'm going through / The trip is not easy / Not told it would be soft and breezy / But God won't walk away / I'm sure to arrive someday / Hold out hope in Him / He's there when the light grows dim / But I'm not tired yet / Not going to whimper and fret / Believe God is the best yet / Never fails to support / That's why I file a good report / Despite some bumps and bruises / Confident in what God uses / Can behold His face / Gives me grace for the race / Fits me for the fight / Victory in sight / Could have been a smoother street / But would not deserve the pilgrim's seat / Now I can keep seeking /

Faith's fuel is not leaking / When I have to stand / God 's always at hand / Promised I would not be alone / Would be there for me when others are gone / Must keep the end in view / To the quest be true / Got His promise to chew / Believe it - I'm going through / I'm going through / Won't be denied / The Lord will provide / What a ride / God at my side / I'm going through / What about you? /

JESUS CRIED, IT'S FINISHED.
"MY DRIVE IS REPLENISHED"

DON'T GIVE UP

I will lift up mine eyes unto the hills, from whence cometh my help. My help cometh from the Lord, which made heaven and earth.
Psalm 121:1-2 (KJV)

Things get a little hard / Can't control your yard / Don't throw in the towel / Curl up and just howl / No victory in submission / Hope is not in remission/ Here's what you got to do / Refocus and get a different view / Not easy to not feel weak / But the answers you must seek / The night may be long and dark / Still you can hit your mark / Secret is to hold your line / Standing straight with a made up mind / God is looking to assess / Are you able to stand the test / Never know what's in store / Reason you must finish your chore / Nobody said it would be easy / Life is not always rosy and breezy / But if you hang in and believe / God is there and won't deceive / It's going to be okay / After night comes the day / Peace is waiting to join you / Just believe that deliverance is due / Nothing's too hard for God / Faith is wonder sod / You can grow / Never feel low / You have a way out / God loves you - no doubt / It's good in the long run / You can be sure it'll get done / That's why you can't fold the tent / Miss your blessing the Master sent / It's all in the will / You can swallow the pill / Though you're hit on the chin / Determination will surely win / Go ahead despite the heat / God's power can't be beat / Life may be a trial / God's watching all the while / Though our steps get slow / Weary legs screaming no / But God is not asleep / Surely will respond and His promises keep / All God needs is your hand / Give it to Him and follow the plan / And win you will / Renewed strength takes the hill / Trouble may plan to disrupt / But the crown is yours / Just don't give up /

YOU ARE NOT MADE WITH A REVERSE GEAR!
GO FORWARD!

THE END ZONE

But he that shall endure unto the end, the same shall be saved.
Matthew 24:13 (KJV)

You must stake your claim / Giving up is a shame / No way you leave the field / It's a game of will / Others are out to stop you / Hold to your vision that's true / Victory can be achieved / It's all about what you believe / It's fighting to advance / Not depending on chance / The end zone is the aim / Marching in His name / Opposition is on the attack / Working to hold you back / It's what your enemy schemes / Assassination of your dreams / His mission is goal prevention / Not bound by any convention / Will stop you at all cost / Driving to be the boss / But you can't falter / Be assertive – don't alter / Struggle is not for the weak / Just know what you seek / Focus on the game plan / Conviction wins the land / Keep your eyes alert / No prize for the inert / Can't afford to sleep / That's guaranteed to make you weep / The game is the thing / Quest for the ring / The end zone is instrumental / Crossing the line is fundamental / Fans are waiting to shout / It's the end zone – on with the rout / Break through and score / Force open the door / There is more in store / The contest is yours to win / Losing focus is a sin / The end zone can be reached again / Faith is never in vain / You did it once – do it twice / Double pleasure is nice / Victory is not offered on a platter / Attitude does matter / Your job is to keep driving / That's the recipe for thriving / End zone demands grit / Stay vigorous – don't quit / The battle is your testimony / Trust God – hold the acrimony / Nobody promised you an easy time / You are still in your prime / The end zone is the winner's domain / It's God's favor – let it rain /

CELEBRATION IS THE PRIZE OF DETERMINATION!

LET YOUR LIGHT SO SHINE

LET IT SHINE

...Let your light shine before others, that they may see your good deeds and glorify your Father in heaven.
Matthew 5:16 (NIV)

Jesus told the story / Show your glory / Don't hide it under a basket / Another name for a casket / Turn up the light / Shine it true and bright / The world must know / Not afraid to show your glow / You have illumination / Show your elation / Light reveals the dark / Truth's arrow hits the mark / No reason to be stingy / Light up the dim and dingy / Use your skill to push His will / Be the light on the hill / Shine like the sun / Put ignorance on the run / Let it shine until darkness is ashamed / Rescuing truth from being maimed / Shine in the dawn / Gentle grace like a fawn / Shine at noon / Casting light like an early moon / Shine at night / Erasing hurt and slight / Shine your light where you are / At home or in the car / Can't let the lamp die / Keep it lit / Fire the sky / Shine all you can / Shame the ugly and give beauty a hand / Shine until hope replaces dope / Truth conquers error / Courage defeats terror / Shine with the Jesus joy / Pure without alloy / Shine in your prayer / Comfort knowing God is there / Shine on the street / Shine in the suite / Shine on all those you meet / Let the glow grow / Light seeds are what we sow / Shine on the road / Peace and love is the code /

All will end up fine / Embracing peace is a positive sign / The world's sin can't malign / Life becomes sublime when we let it shine /

HAVE YOU CHECKED YOUR BATTERIES? BE A HIGH BEAM WITNESS.

JUST BELIEVE

And all things, whatsoever ye shall ask in prayer, believing, ye shall receive.
Matthew 21:22 (KJV)

What's the answer / Afraid of the cancer / Turn to God in trial / He's there all the while / Believe that He is able / His success is no fable / Healing is in His power / Victory even in the darkest hour / Why turn to do this unaided / God's there when dreams have faded / Just reach for His hand / Be still and hear His command / Go forth in confidence / You can leap any fence / The way when gloom is in bloom / Sadness shadowing the room / God is still in control / Has something for the weary soul / Listen to one who can testify / Had a problem to rectify / Felt like it was without hope / Knowledge alone could not cope / Turned to Him in earnest prayer / Found out He would burdens bear / His love did lift and hold / Allowed me to see His Wisdom unfold / Learned that I was really wrong / Needed God all along / Now I have joy to share / Tell the world of His care / Brought me through the terror / Ignoring God is the error / But now I know better / His story's in the Bible Letter / Just believe that prayer answers the dare / Will step up and do its share / It's all in what we think / Doubt and fear will make us sink / Whatever the case / Trusting God is not waste / Hang your faith in Him / He's there when the lamp grows dim / This God won't let you go / An anchor when it's "a tough row to hoe" / Believe that He's serious / Never deserts when things get furious / Glad I found out in time / His joy rings my chime / I am now relieved / The formula is: Just Believe /

BELIEVING IS RAW MATERIAL FOR ACHIEVING

WHAT'S ON OUR MIND

...but be ye transformed by the renewing of your mind...
Romans 12:2 (KJV)

It just don't make sense / Doing stuff that makes us flinch / What's with all the hating / What's wrong with relating / Why we got to have guns that kill / Never knowing peace in His will / What's the matter with us / Filled with anger and lust / Wish we would just chill / Learn to just be still / Life is more than *mine* / Also about what's *thine* / It's got to stop / This scramble for the top / The things that are driving us / Reasons for this fuss / We need to sing a new song / Learn how to get along / End the folly / No shame in being jolly / Man was born to love / Overcome the "push and shove" / Discover a way to embrace / Escape from sin's disgrace / Much better to live in peace / Join hands and extend the lease / Make this world an oasis / Move from sloth and stasis / Reach out to each other / Shame to harm a sister or brother / What pleasure in respect / Much better than neglect / Let's change the direction / Stop the rejection / Try love and affection / It's a better way / Won't wound the day / Offers the best chance / Allows progress to advance / We'll find a great feeling / All about trust and healing / What a wonderful time / Ending ignorance and hate crime / Just know that we can do this thing / Trust, joy, and hope taking wing / Darkness must change address / Can't stay when we confess / God is about caring for us / All He wants is our trust / And this crazy drama will end / No profit in war's sin / It's time for smiles and applause / Love's the right cause /

WHAT YOU THINK WILL CAUSE YOU TO RISE OR SINK! THINK YOUR WAY TO THE TOP.

OPEN THE DOOR

...Eye hath not seen, nor ear heard, neither have entered into the heart of man, the things which God hath prepared for them that love him.
I Corinthians 2:9 (KJV)

Time to turn the knob / Get to your job / Can't stay behind the door / God will go before / Don't quiver in fright / God's got you in His sight / Open the door, please / God can set you at ease / Fear cannot perfect / It lives to reject / Staying inside is deception / Don't fear the world's reception / Open the door with heart / That's the way to start / Cringing in shadows is the devil's trick / His plot is mean and slick / Hung up on doubt is choking / Time for you to get smoking / The moment is yours to choose / Accept it and don't refuse / There's possibility beyond measure / Success will be your pleasure / Don't weight your wings / See what the day brings / Life is your possession / Make it a joyous progression / You must make a move / That's the winner's groove / The universe is your pearl / Success will unfurl / Trust God to provide / But you must decide / Swing it open with a flourish / Confidence will surely nourish / God's love is your assurance / Can't find better insurance / Take the lock off your life / You can triumph over strife / Open the door and inhale / Leave your jail/ Satan is the only one that's mad / That's just too bad and oh so sad / He deserves his frustration / Becoming is your destination / Open the door and sing / You are a child of the King / Been shut up too long / Now it's "forward strong" / Don't waste any more time / Every minute is now prime / Use it for your health / That's spiritual wealth / No need to regret / God's not finished with you – yet / You have possibilities galore / All because you opened the door /

LIFE'S LIMOUSINE IS WAITING. ENJOY THE RIDE.

PLEASE STOP COMPLAINING

Bless the Lord, O my soul,
and forget not all his benefit:
Psalm 103:2 (KJV)

What we got to beef about / We got food and clothes and ain't set out / Got a car to drive and still alive / We always sticking out our hand / Yet last to heed the help others command / Yet we are always beseeching / Time for us to do some inner reaching / God is ready to pour out bounty / Able to do it in every county / But time is ripe for gratitude / Stop our attitude / Be a beatitude / Give God some joy / Stop acting mean and coy / People are more than a toy / Time for us to learn His rule / Dissing others is a fool's tool / We must start sharing our wealth / Aiding others is spiritual health / Just seems the right approach / Obey the Mastering coach / His game plan is sure to deliver / Really loves the true forgiver / Stop our self-praise / No way to earn a raise / It's all about giving thanks / Capital that's richer than all the banks / God's got plenty of money / But that's not what makes the day sunny / What pleases God the most / Being kind to others – burying our boasts / We will really give God a thrill / Find residence in His will / Create ways to do some good / Put some grace in the hood / All we need to do / Change our habits and start anew / God is waiting to send us more than enough / Prizes, baubles and all that stuff / We will never start attaining / If we don't wise up and stop complaining. /

**SPEND MORE TIME AT THE THANKSGIVING WINDOW!
IF YOU THINK ABOUT HIM, YOU HAVE TO THANK HIM.**

NOT TIRED YET

I will lift up mine eyes unto the hills, from whence cometh my help.
Psalm 121:1 (KJV)

The race is not a cakewalk / But I am not going to balk / Know that I have to do my best / Meet the task as a life test / Never give up the fight / Keep running toward the light / Despite traps in my way / Keep striving for a new day / And I'm not tired yet / Won't carp and fret / Know God is the sure bet / Refuse to heed the cynic's advice / Can't stop because it's not nice / Nobody promised it would be clover / Can't stop till it's over / Difficult days may be ahead / Still marching onward – can't play dead / No way that I will cower / Know God's watching from Heaven's tower / Got his gaze upon my progress / Inspires me to deal with duress / Keep focused on the finish / His love Will always replenish / Despite the pain and travail / Still know I can't fail / Content to keep my pace / Hang in to win the race / Sometimes it gets rough / Can't act like a powder puff / Just stick to the path / Face challenges and the enemy's wrath / But I am sure its fine / God's at the end of the line / Got to keep my drive / He's waiting when I arrive / Can't just take a dive / Only the faithful survive / Thus, the trophy is mine to gain / Can't stop whether it's sun or rain / But one thing I know / I'll win - not place or show / No way I'm copping a plea / Can't wait to do my destiny / Convinced that it's in the heart / Conviction is the best part / Won't be scared by holes and pits / Determined if trouble hits / Despite what lies in store / I'm going for more and more / Though days may get cloudy and wet / I am running to beat the sunset / Truth is: I ain't tired yet /

DON'T BE A "DROP OUT"! GO TO THE MOUNTAIN TOP.

TAKE A STAND

And the Lord said unto Cain,
Where is Abel thy brother? And he said,
I know not: Am I my brother's keeper?
Genesis 4:9 (KJV)

It's time to take a stand / Heal the hurt of the land / Can't afford to ignore / Indifference earns a poor score / Called to do serious work / Laziness can't lurk / Bring harmony from discord / Be obedient to the Lord / Discover a way to get along / Stop the threats – try a song / Hatred is not a play thing / Intolerance carries a sting / Judging people by race and skin / It's a mess we are in / Hung up on religion and creed / Blind to pain and need / Interested in doing our "thing" / That has a childish ring / Should stop the bombs and blasts / Shocks which leave us aghast / Time to put down stones / No virtue in broken bones / Violence and terror are drowning our age / Should be ashamed at so much rage / Oh for a little more piety / Establish a loving society / Time to take a stand / Respond to God's command / Stop the finger pointing / Really could use an anointing / Immigration is also an issue / Its solution demands more than brain tissue / Wish we could get it together / It would certainly be fairer weather / What we need is compassion / That's the path to satisfaction / Wiser to seek peace / Stubbornness must cease / Help must increase / There is a task to perform / Takes more than phony charm / It's about creating a good place / Congenial to the human race / Not enough to possess weapons of destruction / Search is on for life construction / Viewing differences is nothing to fear / Understanding is worth a cheer / Must resolve the bias which divides / Create a world where love abides / It's not hard to see / Life ought to be trust and harmony /

YOU CAN DO MARVELOUS THINGS! GET BUSY!

I AM STILL HERE

God is our refuge and strength, a very present help in trouble.
Psalm 46:1 (KJV)

The attack came hard and fast / So much smoke / looked like I couldn't last / But I fell on my knees / Asked God to heed my pleas / Never did throw in the towel / Wasn't scared by the howl / Not about to run scared / Got a secret to be shared / No better help on my side / Surely the Lord will provide / Despite the dark and night / I still got some fight / I'm still here / Nothing to fear / God can bring me cheer / All's well – He's near / I can stay alive / God will arrive / Stop acting depressed / He assures I pass the test / Later for the fuss / I'm not going bust / God is who I trust / King of my life / Leader through angst and strife / Just know it's all okay / Going to last another day / The morning will greet my being / Going forth with new seeing / Though things go awry / No knot God can't untie / Got my faith leaping and twirling / Watching His will unfurling / Just be certain that I won't be beat / No worry about having to cheat / God's eye may be on the sparrow / Also on me when the path gets narrow / So stay up on the news / Not going to lose with what I use / It's God's strength that holds / There for me – won't let me fold / Did look bad for my case / But the Lord made haste / Came to fix my condition / Snatched me from hell and perdition / So I sing my triumph loud and clear / I'm still here /

SINCE YOU ARE HERE, WHAT ARE YOU GOING TO DO?

IT'S TIME TO SOAR

Set your affections on things above, not on things on the earth
Colossians 3:2 (KJV)

Tired of hanging around the ground / Get up and win your crown / Time to get off the floor / Plan for a winning score / Victory won't come to the lazy/ Got to take off when it's hazy / No time to lay around / Such practice ain't sound / Tell you the time is ripe / It's about belief and not hype / The flight plan is filed / Faith's number has been dialed / Really must take to the sky / Visit the height and refuse to die / There's a lot in store / You can have more / Just have faith to the core / Explore higher planes / Get your deserved gains / No reason to deny your good / God's in charge – that's understood / It's time to leave / Got it made if you believe / There's a new life to try / It's waiting in the sky / Nothing comes without vision / Launching out is your decision / God helps those who don't cower / Taking off in His power / Will keep you jetting / Better than watching the sun setting / Time to rise and soar / Got a key to Heaven's door / Everything is in shape / God wears the super cape / His way demands trust / Doubt is soul rust / Time for the faith flight / Voyage to the light / Can't be trapped below / Forfeit Heaven's glow / Blessings are yours to take / God's promises are not fake / You can have what you desire / No need for the muck and mire / There's abundance without measure / God's care is true treasure / Let the storms howl and roar / It's time to soar / Time to soar /

DON'T BE GROUND BOUND! FILE YOUR FLIGHT PLAN.

CHECK OUT YOUR MIND

But the end of all things is at hand: be ye therefore sober, and watch unto prayer.
I Peter 4:7 (KJV)

Hey, how's your day / What you got to say / Time to do it a new way / Can't make it with an old scheme / Just wishing on an empty dream / Got to make a choice / Listen to the inner voice / Better to look inside / That's where it resides / Need to check your mind / Stop living in a bind / That's a path that's blind / Choose a new plan / Take a stand / Become a new being / Time to start seeing / Stop and take stock / Put your life on the clock / Means you can't keep your eyes shut / Stuck in the same old rut / Singing the tune of but—but – but / It's up to you / Grab a new view / There's room at the top / Can get there if you don't stop / Leave the trick behind / Find the new design / It's what you must follow / Fooling yourself is empty and hollow / You can scale the height / Get your goal in sight / No value in alibiing / It's all about trying / It's your chance / Leave your trance / Life's your romance / Don't be lazy / Have faith when things go crazy / Time to really get some drive / You can thrive and arrive / Change your old plot / Get going and untie the knot / It's all about belief / Doing nothing is grief / You get it by sowing / Part of your growing / Get out of your zone / Set a new tone / Put on your war clothes / You can beat the foes / It's your day / Have your say / Check out your mind / New peace you'll find / Check out your mind / You are one of a kind /

YOUR MIND IS A VAULT. KEEP YOUR VALUABLES IN IT!

IN SPITE OF OURSELVES
STOP GIVING GOD A HARD TIME

Then they cried out to the Lord in their trouble, and he delivered them from their distress
Psalm 107:6 (NIV)

Some said I couldn't make it / Cackled that I couldn't shake it / Jeered at my state / Said rescue was too late / Put down my plan / Convinced I was "loser man" / But I kept looking up / Drinking from faith's cup / Would not stop in defeat / Knowing God can complete / Going to hold the hope / Not going back to dope / Don't need the pot / It's just mental rot / Cocaine is insane / Poison and pain / Got to keep my attitude / Stay with rectitude / Correct my error / Excise the terror / Know that I can kick the habit / Run from it like a rabbit / Refuse to whine and cry / No time to alibi / Made my bed of woe / But I got to go / No need to dress in pity / It's down to the nitty gritty / The critics are looking to scorn / View me as tired and torn / But that's their view / They don't have a clue / *The old man* is no more / New man's running the store / Got a charge to finish / Belief won't diminish / Belief will replenish / Must stay in gear / Doubt can't live here / It's freedom time / Stay with my climb / Dare not drop out / Desire is what it's about / Going to break this curse / God is now first / Holder of my hand / Open to his command / Don't have to travel alone / He sets the tone / Gives me support / Salvation is in His report/ Gives me conviction / Life is under His benediction / So I can keep my goal / Find comfort for my soul / It's now a done deal / No pill – just His will / It's coming to pass / His grace will last / Skeptics got nothing to say / I'm walking in a new way / Happy for the discovery / God is chief of my recovery /

GOD IS YOUR BIGGEST BOOSTER. HELP HIM OUT!

IN SPITE OF OURSELVES (PT 2)
STOP GIVING GOD A HARD TIME

0 give thanks to the Lord of lords: for his mercy endureth forever.
Psalm 136:3 (KJV)

We need to get out of the way / God's in charge of the day / Why are we always prancing / Our acts aren't so enhancing / We are into our personal greed / Little attention to the real need/ Always preening on stage / Are we serious about our Age / It's about being real / We must submit to his will / God's plan is often frustrated / We are looking to be celebrated / Always pumping up our chests / Often fail the tests / Full of excuses in crisis time / Don't respond to the bell's chime / We must do more than boast / Stop seeking a self-toast / God really must be cool / Endures us when we play the fool / Know that His patience is tried / Still is there and doesn't hide / God is without peer/ He is kindness bringing cheer / Holds us despite our weakness / Grace shining in the bleakness / Divine Love doesn't neglect / He does provide and protect / Sits high and reaches low / Lifts us above the foe / He keeps on blessing / Let's end the stressing / His love will never fail / Have his promise He will prevail / In spite of our sin / God yet will take us in/ In spite of our doubt / His mercy will bring us out / His gaze never strays / He is the grace of our days / It's truly a gift / His strength gives a lift / In spite of our mishaps / God never naps / Doesn't just turn His back / Still offers what we lack / His love is the real thing / That's a hymn we should sing / In spite of our errors in choosing / God is never confusing / He promises not to disappoint / Offers His favor to anoint / In spite of all we are not / God's love hits the spot / It will cause us to flourish / His truth will always nourish / In spite of ourselves / In spite of ourselves /

IT'S HARD TO FLY WITH WEIGHTED WINGS.
LET'S PLUCK SOME DEAD FEATHERS.

THE HOOD

For in the day of trouble he will keep me safe in his dwelling;...
...I will see the goodness of the Lord in the land of the living.
Psalms 27:5 and 27:13 (NIV)

Raised on the street of trouble / Had enough problems – no singles – all doubles/ Learned how to keep alert / No value in playing hurt / The hood is where I came of age / Learned my lines for life's stage / Told to keep my head high / Copping out is an invitation to die / Believe that one plus one is two / Logic says you get what you're due / It's about playing the rules / Getting by is the game of fools / Hood is just for real / True measure of the will / May be tough soil to sow / Can't evade but must get up and go / Drive with great conviction / The strong survive is the prediction / It's the ground where seeds are planted / Wisdom counsels – take nothing for granted / Don't alibi and give up / Hang-in whatever would disrupt / All you need is some prayer / God is around – call if you dare / See if His help won't provide / Make things better if you decide / Put the project in the Master's care / Knows how to take it from here to there / Hood is really the place / Growth of life by His grace / No need to be defeated by trial / Victory is God assured if you dial / Tell God you are in the hood / Some tried it for evil but all is good / Never believed I was bound for ground / God had me fitted for a crown / Just have to stay intent / Eye on the prize despite the dissent / Hood is not just a dark wood / It's a seed bed to nurture our good / It's really filled with riches and treasure / Birthing ground of boundless measure / So – just know / Put your stuff together and let it grow / The hood's about belief / God awareness is real relief / Started in the hood at birth / It's part of me and soul of my worth / The hood is where it's at / The Genesis moment / Run and tell that /

IT'S NOT WHERE YOU START BUT WHERE YOU FINISH WHICH IS THE MEASURE OF SUCCESS.

TELL ME WHY

Trust in the Lord with all thine heart; and lean not unto thine own understanding.
Proverbs 3:5 (KJV)

Tell me why some dreams fade / Fall apart and don't make the grade / Tell me why / When it looks well / Events go wrong for a long spell / Am I to blame for the mess in the game / Going too fast - ignoring His claim / Did I cause the tower to fall / Listening to everybody but His call / Was it my deaf ear / Reason for the lost cheer / Did I make the bed hard / Playing the game with the wrong card / Tell me why / Some folks live and others die / Some stay on the ground and others touch the sky / Tell me why / Had some plans for promotion / Now my scheme suffered demotion / Thought I had it figured out / But my stuff wasn't stout / Fell apart when the storm came / Nobody but myself to blame / Guess the reason was my blindness / Forgot about love and kindness / So, you want to know why / Listen up / And don't you cry / The end of life isn't money / It's honesty that keeps it sunny / When accounts are low / Integrity will keep the glow / Doesn't matter if you don't have gold / Let the Master's plot unfold / They that wait upon the Lord / Obey His will in sweet accord / Won't miss the prize / Leaning on His arms is wise / I can forsake my sigh / I'll tell you why / Took me a while to perceive / All my troubles came when I conceived / Later for God and didn't believe / The answer is plain for all / Leaving God out will lead to the fall / Holding on to our knowledge / It's okay but it's the wrong college / For our hope is not in our skill / It's being still in His will / Then it won't be any "why's" / God's path is where triumph resides /

LEARNING GOD'S LESSONS
ARE HOW WE PASS LIFE'S TESTS.

I CAN'T SIT DOWN

And let us not be weary in well doing: for in due season we shall reap, if we faint not.
Galatians 6:9 (KJV)

There are places to go / There are seeds to sow / Can't afford to get tired / Must not get mired / Got to travel in double time / Can't relax with a lemon-lime / The task must be completed / Desire can't be defeated / Called for this occasion / Traveling under spirit persuasion / This charge is no easy street / Can't win on the lounge seat / It's a calling to fulfill / Going on even when uphill / Staying attentive to the goal / Look out world, I'm on a roll / Determined to finish the course / Persistence is a mighty force / The Lord's on my side / He surely can provide / It's my role since Christ left / Trust in Him is a strong cleft / God is proud of my drive / His love keeps me alive / There's no power like Him / My comfort when things get dim / Reason why I am confident / My mission is God sent / An individual assignment which identifies / Faith work which glorifies / No way I can take a break / This is not ice cream and cake / Kingdom building is not for the faint hearted / Staying with it once started / Ministry to seek and claim / Working hard honors His name / Lives must be lifted / Committed to the lame and gifted / Called to witness to His truth / His ministry is total proof / Left here to win souls / *Discipling* as life unfolds / This is my season / God knows the reason / I know it's His plan / Never give up on man / Despite the folly of war and hate / Love can still relate / Thus, I can't sit down / Whether others smile or frown / I'm the man from God / It's about Him and not the iPod / The music in my ear is His call / His obedience is worth it all / I can't sit down / At Heaven's graduation – promised my cap and gown / I can't sit down /

AN EASY CHAIR IS NOT ATTACHED TO OUR ANATOMY!

LOVE

START LOVING

For the love of Christ constraineth us;...
II Corinthians 5:14 (KJV)

Stop the shoving / Start some loving / End the killing / Start the healing / Why all the fuss / Must do more than sass and cuss / No way to run a life / World of sorrow and strife / Man must stop hating / Start embracing and relating / Peace is a better style / Just makes more sense all the while / Can't force His will / Result will be void and nil / Better to reason in love / See the flight of the dove / Truth is that it's love's blessing / Always there to start addressing / Love is never on leave / Comfort station when we grieve / On-the-case without fail / Working to make things jell / Trust in love's plan / Only interested in saving the land / Self and pride will divide / Love's house is where to reside / Stop our deceit and conceit / It's love which makes complete / Anger is a waste of time / Crazy as looking for a talking mime / Don't expend strength in folly / Love is joyous as Christmas holly / Keep the temper in check / Losing it causes a wreck / Never give up on love's potion / The communion cup is the right notion / Start loving all we can / Strike up the tune and join the band / Love's the way to wonder / No need to doubt and ponder / The Son came to show the way / Get in a hurry and not delay / Now's the time to sing a love song / Love the right and correct the wrong / It's the season of sharing / Abandon friction and start caring / The joy of love is sublime / Mellow as the tinkle of the wind chime / Let the music touch our heart / Give love a new start / Stop the shoving / Start loving /

A LOVE EMBRACE WILL PUT A CHECK ON DISGRACE.

LOVE

...Now these three remain: faith, hope and love.
But the greatest of these is love.
I Corinthians 13:13 NIV

Love is more than sex / Empty values that only vex / About more than sensation / Really about soul salvation / Love's been cheapened with talk / All posturing and no walk / Love's not an oration / It's all demonstration / You can promise a good game / But backing it up proves your claim / Love's the true thing / Change your day and make it sing / Love will hold and won't fold / Love will bless and meet the test / Love will protect and not defect / Love is strong and long / Love's more than words of a song / Love is what this world needs / A dressing for wounds that bleed / Love will stop the hating / Let trust and respect start mating / Love is more than fluff / It's there when it gets tough / More sublime than rage / It's hate that sours the Age / People must learn to listen / Love's message makes life glisten / Dark clouds shadow the day / Love is the true way / Its love that's real / Worthy of the Master's seal / Need to examine new tactics / Not give in to fanatics / It's a blessed state / Open the gate and negotiate / Love can arbitrate / Put the cards on the table / It's love that's able / Love wants to heal the hurt / Lift dreams from the dirt / It can come to pass / Love can do the task / We are against the wall / Guns and rockets are signs of the fall / Love needs to charge to the rescue / Save the world from its miscue / Love is the answer I tell you / It's what we ought to woo / Love's where it's at / It's hero stuff without the white hat /

LOVE IS MADE FLESH IN YOU!
MAKE LOVE AND NOT CONFUSION.

WHAT CAN WE DO?

And said unto them; Go ye also into the vineyard, and whatsoever is right I will give you....
Matthew 20:4 (KJV)

Why are we standing around / Must work the ground / Hanging at the gate is out / That's not what it's about / There are grapes to pick / Can't ignore the clock's tick / The day is our nut / Crack it and avoid the rut / Go into the fields and shine / We must make the wine / Change the sour to sweet / That's ours to complete / We can embrace the job / Sloth is a thief that will rob / No growth in indolence / It's terrible insolence / We cannot just whine and complain / Desire is the road to attain / Get up and start / It's time to take part / Nothing is achieved through shirking / Put our talent to working / Doing wonders with our drive / Ending lounging and coming alive / What can we do / Get an end in view / Draft a bold design / Our stuff is divine / God gave us more than enough / Shine like diamonds in the rough / Stop fretting about other's gains / Time to break our chains / Refuse to compare our position / It's all about the mind's condition / That's escape from perdition / What can we do / Stay on the case / Remain in the chase / Win the race / Replace doubt with action / That's great satisfaction / Transform the harsh plot / Give it all we got / Irrigate and cultivate /

That's our path to navigate / Keep active in the field / Endurance is part of the drill / Pursue our assignment to the end / It's the way to win / Better to hang in / Overcome whether thick or thin / Crops have to be chopped / Dropping out means we flopped / Staying faithful to the task / Wearing truth's face and no mask / Experiencing a new sensation / Honest effort in the situation / Fooling the skeptics scorn / We harvested the corn / We did go and initiate / Active minds don't vegetate / It's about a growth curve / Just demands vigor and verve / Standing around is out the door / Handling the chore is the path to more / What can we do / Diligence is food to chew / Offers a brighter tomorrow / Can earn and not borrow / Start a new orientation / That's worth conversation / What can we do / To ourselves be true / What can we do / Accept your season – it's due. /

IT'S TIME TO STOP HANGING OUT AND START WORKING OUT!

PRAY ON

Pray without ceasing.
I Thessalonians 5:17 (KJV)

Looks like nobody cares / And nobody shares / Despite the doctor's case / You hold on – still there's grace / Pray on my child / Whether its stormy or mild / Makes no difference what's the weather / God's able to make it better / Can take your life in His hand / Get you to the Promised Land / Pray on and hold fast / Faith and trust will bring it to pass / Practice the prayer gift / Guaranteed to give a lift / Support in the strife / Safety valve for a new life / Never lose your hope / Prayer power can cope / Believe you'll get there / Keep doing your prayer / You won't lose the game / Victory is God's middle name / Let His hand anoint / He's sure and won't disappoint / Just wait upon the Lord / He'll come / Pull the prayer cord / No matter what the test / God provides more – not less / All trials fail to stop / God is bad and is top cop / When the troubles come hard and quick / God alone is my pick / My trust is sure / His grace will surely endure / Don't throw away your blessing / You are going through testing / God only desires this without doubt / Trust in Him for the way out / Pray on for the answer/ Fear is the soul's cancer / Know that God is looking this way / Please Him when you pray / And the day won't be sad / God discovery always makes glad / But know this without excuse / God can put your life to use / Through prayer He's always there / Faith says it's already done / God's real / All else is con / Pray on! / Pray on! /

DON'T WRING YOUR HANDS. LIFT THEM!

GOT SOMETHING TO SAY

...God has called us to live in peace.
I Corinthians 7:15 (NIV)

Got something to say / Can't let it just lay and stay / Need to tell what's on my mind / No profit in pretending I'm blind / Felt the pain of 9-11 / Frustration – ache – troubling my heaven / Guess it woke the dead / First time some of us reflected on the Head / No need to act and pretend / Shook me up not knowing how to contend / But I have gained some direction / Result of deeper reflection / Time's lesson is to stay alert / Awareness lessens the hurt / Truth is we didn't have any "fall back" / Never thought we'd be under attack / Lesson to be learned is harsh / Got to be ready and able to march / Not about just going to war / Really finding out who we are / It's easy to fight back / But tit for tat ain't where it's at / Know that justice must be done / Killing and destruction deserves response / But need to show more than "who's boss" / Such a claim comes at a high cost / Really must be discerning / Satisfy the soul's yearning / Better not stay mad / Devil's trick to keep us "had" / Refuse to buy into "tooth for tooth" / Easy answer that misses the truth / Not enough to show "them" / Manner of life must come from Him / Yes – know it's a burning shame / Yet got to trust in His name / Hard as it appears / Faith is what conquers fears / Want to be about more than getting revenge / Understand that life has been singed / Still love is the way to go / Confidence is what we show / When the world is upside down / Our smiles hidden by a frown / Must still tell the town / Peace making deserves the crown /

LEARNING CAN PREVENT THE BURNING!

THE DOOR

...knock and the door will be opened to you.... and to the one who knocks, the door will be opened.
Matthew 7:7-8 (NIV)

Open the door/ Discover what's in store / Why are you waiting / Stop your hesitating / The answer is beyond the door / Go for it and learn the score / You never win by playing safe / Only your soul will chafe / Go through the door / Be committed to the core / It's alright to explore / Seek for truth and more / Best to get results / Standing frozen only adds insult / Really can't just stop your quest / Truth's inquiry demands the best / Don't be strung out / God's aware of what it's about / Only dare to proceed / Believe Him and never concede / No way it won't work / Can't afford to shirk / All will end up fine / Open the door – make up your mind / Doors are paths to events / Open them with good intent / Never just hang out – facing the floor / If it rains – salt will still pour / Thus, wise up and swing it wide / What you believe can turn the tide / Despite the fear/ His presence has no peer / Keep your ear to the ground / Eye on the crown / Committed to cause despite trouble's roar / Burdens that can make you sore / Still it's true / Believe the Jesus way – join His crew / I know there's a door / No time to snore / And so what if it's thick / Give it a kick / Let out your cry and give it a try / The door may be in your way / Listen to what the Master has to say / All things work for good / Content you did all you could / And you'll learn a great lesson / Pushing ahead gains the blessing /

KEEP KNOCKING! YOU WIN BY PERSISTENCE!

THE START

In the beginning was the Word, and the Word was with God, and the Word was God.
(John 1:1) KJV

Time to really start playing / Answer is really about praying / Self answers can't do the deed / God's input is what I need / Formula and equations are alright / But don't mean much when things get tight / Need more than intellect and brains/ Faith's assistance can break the chains / Not trusting in only what I know / Planting faith seeds will make gardens grow/ When I have tried my best / Not enough to win life's test / Must go another way / Let my God have His say / Just making it hard for no reason / It's yours if God is in season / It's always time to trust in Him / Answers the plight between me an "them" / Enemies can't destroy my plans / I am held in the Master's hands / Need to stop clinging to fears / God's help is what cheers / So go forward with drive / No worrying about those who scheme and jive / I have a winner in the Master / In charge of life's pasture/ Going to make it across the line / Everything is in order – that's divine / So let the issues mount / Know something upon which I can count / Things are not going to fail / Trust in God will excel / Got a fresh surge of power / Comes from Him who is around every hour / Found out that I was weighting my wings / Not asking God earlier is what stings / But now the truth is this / God is glad to assist / Got a smile on my face / Going to win the race / Have joy in my heart / Got God at the start /

GOD IS WHAT YOU SHOULD NEVER LEAVE HOME WITHOUT

MAKE IT REAL

Righteousness keepeth him that is upright in the way: but wickedness overthroweth the sinner.
Proverbs 13:6 KJV

Need to be what you are / You are your own star / No sense in fooling yourself / Take your truth off the shelf / Stop striving to please the crowd / Seek integrity – forget being proud / Stop standing on your wings / Honesty and awareness are the real things / You get what you give / Only do it and start to live / You have kingdoms within you / But to yourself you must be true / No matter what others say / You can make it today / Yours is what you believe / Stepping out is when you achieve / Dare to be a new thought / Old ways are not highly sought / Use your stuff when it gets rough / You can handle it off the cuff / You are able to bring something new / It comes from the inner view / Keep your game in high gear / Honesty is never something to fear / Have your options always clear / Your victory is worth a cheer / Never say that life's too hard / Effort will gain the award / There it is / Just keep the sparkle and fizz / So, keep it real / That's the deal / You can make it with a strong will / All is yours to prevail / Going for it will ring the bell / It's all about the drive to get the prize / You will win while others may be surprised / Make it real / Make it real / You can fill the bill / Climb the hill / Make it real /

A COUNTERFEIT LIFE HAS NO PURCHASING POWER!

HANG IN

because you know that the testing of your faith develops perseverance.
James 1:3 (NIV)

What it be like / That's what I ask / Can you handle the task / Are you up to the job / Can you handle the screams of the mob / Are you on your game when they blame your name / Can you keep the stiff lip / Steer your ship even when fortunates dip / It's not when you fall that's bad / It's staying down and feeling sad / Get up and move ahead / Don't give up and play dead / Stop looking like it's your fault / It's your wall to vault / Don't worry about others' eyes / It's your choice to win the prize / It's not what the folks say / It's your plan that will make a way / What's up with the fear factor / That "ain't" the drama where you ought be lead actor / No matter what comes your way / Hang in / Help is on the way / It's not as if there is no hope / Trusting God is the way to cope / Storms may thunder and roll / Don't throw in the towel and fold / There is a better way / Make it a brighter day / Hang in / Hope will help you win / And when you want to give up / Look up / Gear up / Live up / It's what you choose to do / Backward glance to failed romance / Forward vision with bold decision / Tell you the time is far spent / Don't pay doubt any rent / You got more going for you than concession /

Belief in God is the right confession /And you are sure to win / All you got to do is hang in /

DON'T LET GO! IT'S A LONG WAY DOWN.

DON'T MESS WITH THE WORLD

In the beginning God created the heavens and the earth.
Genesis 1:1 (KJV)

Our world is a gift / Given to offer a lift / A stage of wonder / Depth to ponder /A place to nourish / Its abundance to cherish / Need to offer thanksgiving / Just practice responsible living / Conduct our tenure with nobility / Exercise deepest humility / It's up to us not to pollute / Better to choose a wiser route / Realize we did not buy the land / It comes from the Master's hand / It's ours to maintain / Yet we fuss and complain / It's not about our turf / God gave us the whole earth / This is our blessing / Time to stop the messing / Need to go another way / Bring some sanity today / People must stop the fighting / It's God's will we are slighting / It's time to save our age / Be still and end the rage / God gave the world for peace / Time for violence to cease / It's a venue for hope / Must be wise and not a dope / Embrace the present hour / Gain perspective from truth's tower / Given a chance to change and perfect / It's crazy to reject / Must put our minds to work / It's ignorance where danger lurks / We can make the world better / We can help the weather / Stop the global warming / That's harming which ain't charming / Called to the kingdom for such a time as this / Transform ugliness into bliss / Choose a different scheme / Realize the dream / Filling the world with care / That's for all to share / Keeping the goal in view / Love for all – not the few / The world is not just for the rich / Truth must make its pitch / What good is dominating wealth / Concern is about total health / False profit in gouging the oil / Just makes tempers boil / Honor should not be hanged / Our practices must be changed / This is God's place / End the disgrace/ Come to the table / Discover God is able / He wants us to try kindness / Erase moral blindness / Begin a new thing today / Being our brother's keeper is the way / It would end world weeping / That's worth shouting and leaping /

THE WORLD IS YOUR HOUSE.
HOW'S YOUR HOUSE KEEPING?

MOUNTAINS ARE MADE FOR CLIMBING

SPEAK TO YOURS

THE BALL IS IN YOUR COURT

I have set before you life and death, blessing and cursing: therefore choose life, that both thou and thy seed may live.

Deuteronomy 30:19 (KJV)

Play the game / Up to you to stake your claim / The ball is in your court / Act now or your dreams abort / Get off your bench / Got to go and not flinch/ Need to take a stance / This is your chance / Not wise to pass the buck / Life's more than luck / Got to show some pluck / Opportunity can't be ducked / Grab a piece of the action / Gain some traction / Never look back with regret / Choice is yours to go and get / You are called to compete / Stay the course and complete / No points for hand sitting / You lose by quitting / Either you will or won't / You do or don't / The choice is yours to make / Which road you will take / Tell you this though / Must not be so slow / The world needs your skill / It's success in the Master's will / Trust that won't retreat / Faith in God can't be beat / You really don't have to fear / God will help – that's clear / But God won't break in / Opening the door is the way to win / Why are you looking all confused / Seeming bemused and misused / You have the best hand / Can't lose under God's command / Step between the lines / God's for you – don't whine / Advance to the net / Head scratching will make you fret / And you will be surprised / The best plan is God devised / It was always in the bag / Being scared was a drag / Now the day is really sweet / Won your game – what a feat / Think how much time was lost / Not trusting God is high cost / Now you can leap and scream / Wasn't as bad as it seemed / Never sell yourself short / Call God when the ball's in your court /

FAITH IS THE SWEET SPOT ON YOUR RACQUET! HIT THE BALL!

CAT GOT YOUR TONGUE

...therefore choose life, that both thou and thy seed may live:
Deuteronomy 30:19 (KJV)

It's time to raise your voice / Better make your choice / No sense in keeping quiet / That's an empty diet / Must speak with conviction / Don't muffle your diction / Opinions are a declaration / Take a stance with no hesitation / Afraid to give an expression / That's just mind suppression / Share what you feel / That's keeping it real / Don't sit on your view / It's all about to thyself be true / When the question comes your way / You can have your say / Don't be numb with doubt / You can make your shout / "Cat got your tongue" is a sign of fright / Being scared blocks the light / Saying it out is what it's about / Demonstration of courage – that's clout / It's giving your perspective / All right to be reflective / It's fence sitting that's defective / Standing up is effective / Elijah charged the crowd / Don't cower – say it loud / Choose who you'll serve / Just requires some nerve / Playing safe is a shame / It affronts God's name / Wavering and not selecting / That's a practice worth rejecting / The people didn't say a word / But they weren't deaf and surely heard / The prophet was incensed / They had no defense / But he made his witness / Demonstrated soul fitness / Called the fire from Heaven / Faith is the true leaven / Don't let the "cat" work its plan / It's all in God's hand / You are the star of this story / Choosing God is great glory / Elijah's charge is yet alive / Being decisive will let you thrive / "Cat got your tongue," is pure fiction / Claiming God is the real benediction /

YOUR TONGUE DOES NOT NEED A YELLOW STREAK AS A FASHION ACCESSORY.

GO FOR THE GOLD!

...and let us run with patience the race that is set before us,
Hebrews 12:1 (KJV)

Go for the gold / Be strong and bold / Success is staying in the race / That's a winner's place / It's not always finishing in front / But it's dropping out that's a loser's stunt / Be faithful to your vision / Maintain that with precision / Never throw in the white flag / Surrender is not your bag / Bowing to defeat / No way to compete / Christ rewards the desire / The passion of a soul on fire / A vigor that keeps driving / Commitment to thriving / Fighting off the fatigue / That's really major league / Running for the finish line / Focusing on the Master Mind / Refusing to stop for a break / This contest is no fake / Demands attention to task / After the race is the time to bask / Have to turn it up a notch / Can't afford to botch / Keep pressing for the prize / That's a habit that's wise / Going on in Jesus' name / No quit in His game / He set the style for attitude / It's not just aptitude / Believing in his will / Always fills the bill / Medals are a byproduct / Christ is into your conduct / It's running with resolve / Fear can't dissolve / The race is a symbol of life / All about defeating strife / Redouble the will to win / It's giving up that's the real sin /

**24 CARAT IS NOT JUST ABOUT JEWELRY!
IT LOOKS GOOD ON YOUR MIND!**

JUDGMENT

...if man be overtaken in a fault, ye which are spiritual, restore such an one in the spirit of meekness;...
Galatians 6:1 (KJV)

Seems easy to point the finger / Judging others with a sharp zinger / Putting people down in a harsh manner / Self-righteousness waving its banner / But we should be careful in condemnation / Don't always know the situation / Surface events may not be the whole story / Confusion may shield some glory / Nobody is beyond mistakes / Be sensitive for goodness sakes / Jesus warns against finding fault / Better bring intolerance to a halt / His lesson is for us all / Fault finding is truly small / It's no virtue in denigration / Character assault is devastation / Wiser for us to hold the stone / Who is not error prone /All of us have come short of the mark / Life is more than a lark / Experience teaches restraint / Things sometimes look what they "ain't" / Need to hold our barbs / May land some in psych wards / Fragility makes others pain / Ought to let them explain / No merit in quick disdain / We should not look for the speck / Grabbing others by the neck / It's clear we all have foibles / May seem we have lost our marbles! We should cancel the "thumbs down" / Jesus has come to town / Appears with grace and love / Wisdom from above / Speaks to the criticized / Gives audience to the ostracized / His nature is to forgive / Just wants us to learn to live / Stop denying others kindness / Turn from our ignorance and blindness / His way is affection / Too caring for rejection / He gave His life / Sacrifice to end the strife / Time to acknowledge our commonality / We all share carnality / Jesus' love is sublime / He erased our spiritual crime / Now is the time to declare / End our judgment with a love affair / A relationship of humility / A union of civility / Christ calling for caring / Embracing truth and sharing / Put an end to the blame game / Understanding honors His name /

JUDGMENT IS A BOOMERANG. LOOK OUT!

WHAT WE NEED

Delight thyself also in the Lord: and he shall give thee the desires of thine heart.
Psalm 37:4 (KJV)

The world has bling and everything / Evidence of our striving / Inventions and gadgets fill our space / Still not the answer for the human race / More to it than a pimped up ride / Really is based on what the Lord can provide / We revel in a lot of stuff / But we can't cope when time gets tough / Know we believe it's about the cash / Feeling good about our stash / Not here to put down money / But people still act funny / They'll hang when the party is popping / Interested in bopping and copping / But when the set is over / They are looking for another four leaf clover / We must look beneath the cover / That's where we find a true lover / More than any current trend / Can't beat a caring friend / One that will stay with us / A rock we can trust / A comfort when things are down / Present whether it's a smile or frown / Stays by our side / Helps us ride out the tide / What we need is food for the soul / Nourishment to keep us whole / Strength for the course / A real resource / Stamina for the run / Assurance 'til day is done / Friendship that's true and pure / Support that will endure / Steady advice in stress / Assistance in winning the test / A call to offer cheer / That's concern which is precious and dear / We need eyes to help us see /

Follow the path to liberty / Hands to share the load / Guidance on the road / Wisdom to make the choice / Ears to hear his voice / Humility to be still / Obedient to His will / What we need is love that won't get cold / Vibrant when we grow old / Love that is our hope / Holds us on the slick slope / Yes, we need friends for life / Got our backs in strife / On this celebration of love / Stay focused on things above / Don't let your light grow dim / It's all about the peace that's found in Him / What we need / I'll share my creed / In our period of travail / The Lord will prevail / What we need / It's Christ who can lead / What we need / Through Him we shall succeed /

ADDRESS YOUR NEEDS. YOUR WANTS CAN WAIT!

HOLD IT STEADY

...therefore have I set my face like a flint, and I know that I shall not be ashamed.
Isaiah 50:7 (KJV)

(In Tribute to Dr. Martin Luther King)

He didn't cut and run / Never stopped when they schemed to shun / Knew His calling was sure / Just hung in to endure / Kept the focus on his role / Freedom and justice was the goal / Wasn't in for the praise / Not called to be the latest craze / The King man was not playing / Hitched his belt and kept praying / Could have given up / Spat out the dregs of a bitter cup / In this season of ferment / His sacrifice shouts: "He was sent" / Martin stayed the course / Disciple of the Love Force / Walked even when troubled / Stood when resistance doubled / Called to the Kingdom to minister / Fight against plots mean and sinister / Would not bow and scrape / Never attempted to escape / His efforts were inspired / We can't get tired / Racism and Hatred got to go / Time for justice seeds to sow / Now is the time / Doing nothing is a crime / The drum major had to lead / His vision was to meet the need / So join in praise of Dr. King / Lift our voices: Let freedom ring /

FEAR HAS NO PLACE AT THE SHOW DOWN!

WHO SAID SO

(For we walk by faith, not by sight:)
II Corinthians 5:7 (KJV)

Who said I couldn't make it / Had to give up – couldn't take it / Just proves they don't know whose I am / Got an ace when it's a jam / Friend who got my back / Never leaves when under attack / Just know I'm going to gain the prize / Always watched by His eyes / Heed the counsel of His Word / Never forsake - haven't you heard / Trust in His power / Brings you through the darkest hour / All is going to work out / The Master's love is strong and stout / Covers me like a cloak / Solid as an oak / Just need to be still / Not mine but His will / Don't know how it's done / Yet He's there when the day is run / Company for the long night / Freed from fear and needless flight / God's game is what I got / Always in time – right on the dot / Have true joy and hope / Nothing's too hard to cope / No error in His lesson / Faith is the blessing / Committed despite the test / God's love is the best / It's your winning seal / He's in charge – power to heal / Keep your head to the sky / All about faith that won't die / Despite how it seems / Got to heed the Master's schemes / Follow His code and creed / Look to Him – fulfill the need / Just plant the seed / The crops will grow and flourish / His love does nourish / Can't stop from shouting / His plan is worth touting /

It's no way that Satan can win / God's with us from front to the end / Forget those who spoke defeat / My Lord still sits in the Ruler's seat / Who said no / They didn't know / Got God / Let's go /

PEOPLE MAY TALK AND DOUBT.
GOD ALONE HAS REAL CLOUT.

STRONGHOLD

(For the weapons of our warfare are not carnal, but mighty through God to the pulling down of strongholds;)

II Corinthians 10:4 (KJV)

Took a dare and tried the stuff / Never thought it could get rough / Was I in for a shock / It really made my world rock / Always thought I was in charge / Knew how to live it large / But I put weights on my life / Now burdened with trial and strife / Something I never believed / No way I could be deceived / But I fell into a trap / Lured by the devil's map / Things looked so exciting / The sweet life - no nail biting / Enticed by play and pleasure / Convinced I found my treasure / I ran around night and day / Made every scene without delay / Stayed until the party was over / I was midnight rover / Burning my candle bright and fast / Foolish formula that couldn't last / Soon discovered I was in a rut / Really hit me in the gut / Thought I could get off the merry-go-round / It kept moving – I was bound / My world became sour and gray / Darkness flooded my day / It was a grim outlook / Truth was I was hooked / Thought I was in control / Now shivering from the cold / Satan's scheme is slick / Pretends it's healthy and not sick / But when you try to disconnect / Deny him and defect / That's when you learn / Satan blocks every turn /

He has you in his hold / Always plotting for your soul / And he shakes with glee / Certain of victory / But Christ offers His hand / "Come to Me" / Got a better plan / Just tell the devil to get lost / I have paid the cost / Stand up to his bluff / Let him huff and puff / There's nothing he can do / I am looking out for you / Strongholds only hold the weak / I am refuge for all who seek / You can break his grip / Accepting Me is really hip / Tell strongholds to get back / "My grace is the right track" / I found that Christ does not fail / Satan's hold is not my jail /

**THE DEVIL IS NOT THE BADDEST GUY IN TOWN.
CHRIST IS!**

GOD CAN HANDLE IT

...Be strong...; be not afraid,... for the Lord thy God is with thee whithersoever thou goest.
Joshua 1:9 (KJV)

I am starting this day / Seeking the more excellent way / Some may boo and hiss / But I do know this / It's Your will that I persist / You desire my trust / Your promises are true and just / Must stay on my task / You are there when I ask / It's Your Word that gives life / You are present in strife / You are the God of relief / It's in you I have belief / Despite the challenges that mount / There's refreshing at your fount / Your peace never fails / It's deliverance that prevails / It's a joy to proclaim / I win in Your name / I Walk with a straight back / There's nothing You lack / I have the assurance / Faith is the premium for my insurance / Don't have to spend time in doubt's prison / You are the safety bag in collision / Confident that victory shall be mine / You are my bread and wine / Happy that You watch the sparrow / Your vision is not narrow / You see me in my need / You water my seed / Allows hope to grow / Won't let me get too low / Lifts me from the ditch / Tunes me to your pitch / Brings order to my world / Calms the storm's swirl / Holds me in your arms / Safety from crises and alarms / No way I change loyalty / You are the only royalty / You are the King of kings /

Decreeing good whatever life brings / Your grace is always sufficient / Can't be deficient / Your will is the seal / No hurt You can't heal / I can rest in Your grip / I'm not afraid on the trip / Accepting You is good sense / You are my God and defense /

GOD IS THE ONE TO CHOOSE. NO WAY YOU CAN LOSE.

STEP UP TO THE PLATE

...I heard the voice of the Lord, saying,
Whom shall I send, and who will go for us?
Then said I, Here am I; send me.
Isaiah 6 8 (KJV)

You can get a hit / You just can't sit / Stand up and get a bat / It's really where it's at / Take your practice cuts / Leave your ruts and buts / You have success in your swing, / Connecting is a sweet thing / It's about standing at the plate / Be on time and not late / Meeting the test / Handling pressure and stress / Striking out is not something to fear / God is always near / It's not going to be a home run every time / Refusing to bat is the crime / But your charge is to try / Never give up with a sigh / Keep your eye on the ball / Knock it off the wall / If you fly out instead / You are still alive and not dead / Get it the next time up / You can yet drink from the champion's cup / Now is your chance / Keep the forward glance / Your destiny is at hand / Success is still in the land / Be vigilant in your quest / It helps when Christ is your guest / Focus with resolve / Your commitment won't dissolve / You can achieve your goal / Stay in your role / It's your opportunity / It rhymes with importunity / Remain focused on your scheme / Never sacrifice your dream / Keep digging in / You will surely win / Hold your head high / It's yours now

– not in the “sweet bye and bye” / Reward is for those who don’t fold / Stay firm, strong, and bold / Stay your course / God is the Force / This is your turn at the plate / Don ‘t vacillate / Your God is first rate /

GOD IS THE HITTING COACH.
PRACTICE WHAT HE TEACHES.

ON GUARD

Behold the fowls of the air: for they sow not, neither do they reap, nor gather into barns; yet your heavenly Father feedeth them. Are ye not much better than they?
Matthew 6:26 (KJV)

God is on the throne / Call Him on the faith phone / Don't need to send Him a text / No need for a pretext / Just tell God our condition / Belief is great ammunition / Resource to wage the fight / Never deserts in the night / Enemies don't take a break / Almost more than we can take / But God said to stay on track / He has no lack or slack / Be still and know / He never fails to show / He will come when we are in need / Doesn't want us to ache or bleed / Just offers us a cure / Trust Him and endure / Focus on his wonder / We're going over – not under / Loves us for His name's sake / Trouble for Him is a piece of cake / He is a help in trial / Put Him on automatic dial / Stands ready to appear / Thrilled to erase the fear / Watches over life's journey / He's there from cradle to gurney / Look to Him for peace / His love won't cease / His promise does not trick / God is never slick / His majesty is not a sham / His "I Am" beats the jam / His skill fills the bill / His motto is: Be still / God's the Chief / Has an answer for every beef / Must trust His perception / Ignoring Him is foolish deception /

He is awaiting our call / His assurance won't let us fall / Seek Him while we can / Let Him take our hand / He's a guide that knows the frail / His presence will never fail / All things can be resolved / His assistance must be involved / Conquest will be our reward / Victory is certain: God's on guard! /

THE NATIONAL GUARD AND/OR THE MARINES DON'T HAVE A PATENT ON GUARD DUTY.

IT'S YOUR CALL

I call heaven and earth to record this day against you, that I have set before you life and death, blessing and cursing: therefore choose life, that both thou and thy seed may live:
Deuteronomy 30:19 (KJV)

Decisions are yours to make / You decide the stance to take/ It's up to you / To yourself be true / No reason to give in / You must choose to win / Don't have to concede / Just take the lead / It's your call / Scale the wall / No more stalking defeat / It's a journey to complete / Despite the doubt / Belief is what it's about / I tell you this / Never fear the risk / It's your call / So what if you fall / Your game is your plan/ It's in your hand/ Step out and make your move / Stay in a positive groove / No need to weight your wings / It's your call to do a new thing / The reward goes to the seeker / Hesitation just makes you weaker / God offers blessed strength / Not worried about the journey's length / Firm up your knees / Be sure, He hears your pleas / Your goal is in view / But it's still up to you / Don't go into a stall / Struggle takes guts and gall / God certainly will aid / Still your mind must be made / You won't be left alone / Grace is close as the prayer phone/ Reach out and take charge / No challenge is too large / It's really your call / Time to play ball / You can win the game / Your team bears the Master's name / You have the code for success / It's your zest to be the best / God's glad to protect / Just be constant and don't defect / Keep telling you / You're in God's view / God is able / Can run the table / At your house or at the mall / God can / It's your call / It's your call /

NO REASON TO STALL. GOD SAYS YOU WON'T FALL!

WE DON'T KNOW

If any of you lack wisdom, let him ask of God, that giveth to all men liberally, and upbraideth not; and it shall be given him.
James 1:5 (KJV)

More to it than we don't know / That answer ain't got no glow / Can't just throw up our hands / Perplexed looks *ain't* what life demands / Need to get our act in line / Come alive and use our minds / Shame to respond: to stop or go / Shrug our shoulders that we don't know / We have the assignment / It's a major consignment / No wisdom in scratching our heads / Got to strategize or wake up dead / People who want to thrive and grow / Can't shuffle and moan that we don't know / It's up to us to wage the war / Shoot for the highest star / No failure in belief / Confidence gives relief / All we have to do / Take the inside view/ There's a reward waiting / Need for meditating / Discover pride in our stride / Bold reaching because God's on our side / Can't shame God's assistance / Stuck in uncertainty is resistance / Why are we hanging our hope / Stumbling blindly like we can't cope / What's up with standing still / Talking about "that's a tall hill" / God won't leave us / Our future won't be dust / That's why seeds we must sow / Better path than we don't know / Be clear that God never lies / His word is fail proof – never dies / No sense in standing in a quandary / Minds in need of a spiritual laundry / Why we look so strange / God will provide and won't change / Tell you it's our game / Go on in His name / And no longer must we shrug / Get out of the hole we dug / Got a new approach for living / A recipe that keeps on giving / Don't have to take low and sing woe / Free from the epitaph we don't know /

DON'T JUST KNOW YOUR ABCs.
LEARN ABOUT GOD, IF YOU PLEASE.

THE WORLD IS AT YOUR FINGERTIPS

MASTER MIND

But my God shall supply all your need according to his riches in glory by Christ Jesus.
Philippians 4:19 (KJV)

God is our supply / Must live and not die / Time to try a new thing / Leave winter for spring / Shed the chains that bind / Walk with the Christ mind / Experience revelation glee / Embrace our destiny / No more excuses and reasons / It's celebrating glory seasons / Offered a moment to choose / Why would we refuse / Called to be aware / Faith can address every dare / Occasion for achievement / No cause for bereavement / Given a chance to glow / Recognition is how we grow / Seize the day / End the delay / Seek the more excellent way / Open hearts can receive / It's ours if we believe / It's not nuclear science / Christ is reliance / He's mind that guides / The Lord surely provides / No way to go alone / He reigns on the throne / Awaits our requests / Assurance for our tests / Why be uptight / There's still some light / We walk with hope / No time to grope / Wise to rise / Time to devise / God is all we need / It's in the Book – just read / Promises He won't fail / Never leaves us in jail / Liberates us for our good / His truth is understood / Not our virtue that's so pure / God's help is the cure / Better to conduct a check / Minus God – it's all a wreck /

A REAL FIND IS DISCOVERING THE CHRIST MIND

THE KING MAN

...Go ye, and tell that fox, ... I must walk to day, and to morrow,... for it cannot be that a prophet perish out of Jerusalem.
Luke 13:32-33 (KJV)

King, King, he's our man / Took things in hand / Called the people the beloved community / Developed a design for unity / Not about our complexion / Concerned about our direction / We look to the Memphis motel / Not the Hilton or Swissotel / But it was the balcony of Loraine / When things just went insane / The King of love was slain / Victimized by the ignorance of Cain / Yet the trumpet still sounds / His truth yet making its rounds / Walk together children / Though you get teary / God won't let you get weary / We have the commission to realize / Work the plan – and visualize / Time to stay in the race / Keep a steady pace / Know like King that God is our ace / So, here we are in 2018 / King's commitment retains its sheen / We honor his life and duty/ Transcending ugliness with noble beauty / Yes, we give a shout out / His name we tout / Martin Martin, he's our hero / Never was a moral zero / He did the disciple thing / Let his actions take wing / Heeded the summon to lead / Undaunted that he might bleed / We are richer by his work / He marched where danger lurked / Must fulfill the dream / Manifest the scheme / We dare not sit and sleep / We must get busy and reap / We are the heirs of spiritual wealth / Left to nurture our souls' health / Up to us to cultivate and irrigate / Time is on us – can't be late / Must not hibernate / Go forth and activate/ King, King, he's our man / The drum major leading the band /

COURAGE IS WHAT YOU EXHIBIT WHEN YOU REFUSE TO SUBMIT TO FEAR AND RESIGNATION.

AIN'T GOING TO TURN AROUND

And ye shall be hated of all men for my name's sake: but he that endureth to the end shall be saved.
Matthew 10:22 (KJV)

The business of living ain't always easy / Can get choppy and things turn queasy / You may get slapped down by life / Troubled and going under the knife / But don't turn around / Stand your ground / Keep striving for the crown / What good is it to hang your head / Crawl in a box and play dead / God says you are better than that / Keep moving and don't stand pat / You are more than a complaint / God loves the committed saint / Trials may plot to turn you back / But you can make the counterattack / Know that God's eye sees more than the sparrow / Makes a way when it's narrow / Stay the course and keep your gait / May not come soon – but he's never late / Firm up your will / You can climb the hill / Can't do it if you whimper and sigh / Give up and start to cry / Tell you there's a way through / Just hang in – His Word is for you / Yield not to sleep / Time to rise and leap / Let go of the comfort zone / God's with you – stone to the bone / It's all about trust / It sustains when success becomes dust / Whatever the forecast of gloom / Not going to get trapped in doom / There's light for the room / Garments woven on His loom / Dressed for the full trip / Going on at a steady clip / And one thing that causes mirth / Glad I share the new birth / Though struggle is not over / He's surer than a four leaf clover / Got the thrill of conquest / His love wins the contest / Glad to say it loud and proud / Not ashamed to tell the crowd / God really is the reason / I'm having a spring season / Ain't going to turn around / Know His way is strong and sound / Can't turn around / He scents my track like Heaven's hound / Can't turn around / I'm not lost but found / Can't turn around / Refuse to lose ground /

A BACKWARD FOCUS CAN LEAD TO A FORWARD FLOP.

DREAM YOUR DREAM

Jesus said unto him, If thou canst believe, all things are possible to him that believeth.
Mark 9:23 (KJV)

It's your dreams to do / All about goals and you / Don't stop your quest /it's about being the best / Others don't see the road / Not aware of the load / You must stay on your toes / Faith and desire defeat all foes / You are what you think / Doubt's weight will make you sink / Believe what you can be / Time to forge a new destiny / You are God's grand creation / Got a story to tell the nation / it's a vision for success / Going on to pass the test / Never give up your plan / You are the cream of the land / No way you can fail / Just trust in God – all hail / Keep your face toward tomorrow / Be hopeful – later for sorrow / No regret in just being you / Nobility rests in being true / All things are for your good / Making it right – understood / Your day rings the chimes / What a lesson for these times / Now it's your story / Bright access to truth and glory / Know that this is your choice / Your moment to raise your voice / Reward your action / Taste the joy of self-satisfaction / Now the race is not so harsh / Thanks for lighting the torch / The trophy is your mark / Symbol of defeating the dark / Now is your hour / Going in the Master's power / New creations poised to prance / Grand designs that enhance / It's your prize / "Grit to git" was always in your eyes / So lift your Oscar high / You did well, never said die / It's been dark in the valley / Faith led the rally / It's been a long trip / Raise the cup / Take your sip /

DON'T PERCH IN THE PIT.
THE MOUNTAIN TOP IS WHERE YOU SHOULD SIT!

KEEP CLIMBING

Know ye not that they which run in a race run all, but one receiveth the prize? So run, that ye may obtain.
I Corinthians 9:24 (KJV)

Know the path is long / Just persist and be strong / No matter how tough it is / Faith answers life's quiz / Battle scars are what we earn / Not dropping out is a lesson to learn / Be convinced of the way / No matter what others say / The issue is the Master's will / The boost to take the hill / Don't care if the mountain's tall / No matter whether it's large or small / All He desires is our trust / Put Him first is a must / Keep your faith in gear / No way that God's not near / Don't retire when it gets rough / Life's voice seems harsh and gruff / You must never to give in / The believer wins because Christ is our kin / Despite the slipping and sliding / Never fear: God's yet providing / Don't look for pity / Courage in Him takes the city / Let the clouds grow heavy with rain / You can still make the gain / No reason to act frightened / He always will enlighten / Your strength is with God / Power is in His staff and rod / So step up your pace / Finish the race / Despite the steep ascent / Hang in and don't relent / Truth be told / Be bold and don't fold / Following God is a test of the soul / So, put some stiffening in your back / Sharpen your mind – follow the truth track / Never stay in bed / No way to get ahead / Refuse the cop out / Time to top out / Go forward with drive / God's love can revive / The struggle tests your heart / But stand up and start / Run to meet your fate / God's on time and never late /

THE MOUNTAIN IS NOT MOVING. BUT YOU NEED TO!

CAN'T KEEP QUIET

...Clap your hands all ye people; shout unto God with the voice of triumph.
Psalm 47:1 (KJV)

And he answered and said unto them, I tell you that, if these should hold their peace, the stones would immediately cry out.
(Luke 19: 40) KJV

Got something to shout about / God's love brought me out / Saved me when I was in doubt / Reached me at my lowest ebb / Freed me from despair's web / Lifted me to a higher plain / Took me from loss to gain / Showed me a new road / Helped me carry the load / When I think about God's care / His peace and love I must share / Never did He put me down / Was patient when I was a clown/ I was a big fool / Dropped out of school / Never used my mind as a tool / But God kept me going / Offered me a chance for growing / Nobody knows the trouble I've seen / God's grace is great and pristine / What a great God we serve / He's there when life tosses a curve / Won't let you lose your nerve / Helps you act with vim and verve / No way I can keep quiet / Praising God is my daily diet / He brought me from negation / Gave me hope and affirmation / Now I stand on table land / Brought here by the Master's hand / Who wouldn't give God props / In my book – He's tops / Really have a story to tell / Caught me when I fell / What can I tell you / He won't let me be blue / When things were askew / His Word made it new / Consoled me for the journey / Saved me from the morgue's gurney / What a reason to raise my voice / Tell everybody God's my choice / He was there when others left / Felt sad and bereft / But found His love to be real / Better than a pill / It's the Savior's seal / Can't act reserved / God is well deserved / Look at me praising like I lost my mind / Not giving God thanks would be dumb and blind / God is special without doubt / That's why I must shout / He knows what it's about /

I REFUSE TO LET SOME STONES MAKE MORE NOISE FOR GOD THAN I CAN.

SING YOUR SONG

And he hath put a new song in my mouth, even praise unto our God: many shall see it, and fear, and shall trust in the Lord.
Psalm 40:3 (KJV)

Ought to have a song / Fortress when things go wrong / Something to keep you going / Support for you in seed sowing / Push toward tomorrow / Got your back – despite loss and sorrow / No profit in defeat / God can keep you on your feet / Look to the Master / He leads through disaster / Sing your song of belief / Speaking faith gives relief / Let the world know / Darker it gets – more you glow / Nothing beats the Son / Christ's love will get it done / Let the truth rise and shout / God loves you – don't pout / Reason to keep singing / God is calling – my phone's ringing / Got a message of peace / It's easy when I release / Keep God on speed dial / Always there despite Satan's guile / Keep singing your song / Words cheer and make strong / A torch in the gloom / Radiance flooding the room / Fragrance chasing the stench / God is there in the pinch / Got this challenge beat / God is an umbrella in the heat / Will keep me in the shade / Gives me joy – I made the grade / Sing my song loud and clear / His comfort beats the fear / Truth is my protection / God's love is authentic affection / No reason to act confused / Won't be misused or bemused / Going to keep my aim / No blame in His name / Triumph is what I got / God provides my slot / Meet the day strong / Sing your song / Sing your song / Praise God / He's never wrong / Unshakeable resource all day long / Sing your song /

YOUR LYRICS ARE YOUR LIFE. KEEP COMPOSING!

FREEDOM TO BE ME

If the Son therefore shall make you free, ye shall be free indeed
John 8:36 (KJV)

You have released me to thrive / Must not lose my drive / Gave me space to soar / Chance to do more / Brought me to where I belong / Forgave me when I was wrong / Place to sing my song / Removed my fear of action / Your goodness is the main attraction / Now is the hour of celebration / Certain of my destination / Called to the Kingdom for this hour / Demonstration of divine power / Liberated from foolish fear / Pointless since God is near / Answer in every case / Just seek His face / Up to me to advance / This is my best chance / Granted talent to achieve / Only believe / I can become better / Faith flies in any weather / Cannot be grounded / Refuse to be hounded / It's a matter of will / Empowered by His zeal / Never leaves me stranded /Always around when the crowd has disbanded / Nurtures me with His support / Assured of a good report / Unfazed by negative criticism / Covered in His optimism / Rising in greater flight / Secure in divine might /

DOING THAT WHICH IS BECOMING IS NEVER UNBECOMING

MY FRIEND

Greater love hath no man than this, that a man lay down his life for his friend.
John 15:13 (KJV)

Leads me through night fright / Sure got a real friend / Covers me like a mother hen / And when trials test my core / He calms me and knows the score / No need to worry / Get upset and in an hurry / My dreams are mine to achieve / Trust my Friend and believe / Despite the noise and din / It's all cool / I've got my friend / He doesn't pretend / Sticks with me while I'm on the mend / Holds me when it's mad and crazy / Days cloudy and things hazy / Still have the best hand / The Master is top command / He's my friend / Will bring it out in the end / Sure to win / On Him depend / Never have to fear / God is handy and near / He gives me words of cheer / "I am" is precious and dear / He's my friend / The one I recommend / Others may curse and offend / Try to make me bend / I have a sense of God's desire / His will is that I don't expire / He has new life to energize / Stays close that I may realize / Can make it if I visualize / He desires that I mobilize / Tells me to get up and actualize / He's my friend / When sirens cry loud and shrill / Just be calm in His will / He's got it all mapped out / Plan for living is what it's about / Just trust Him and don't doubt / I can TKO in my bout / His eye is upon me /

Holds me close for victory / My friend won't trick / Keeps me steady when the road is slick / Don't know where I would be / If my Friend wasn't there, you see / I know this without quibble / I always find some truth to nibble / He's such a prized buddy / Always able even when it's wet and muddy / His loyalty won't fade / With Him, I've got it made / He turns up the light / His love conquers every plight /

FRIENDSHIP IS THE BEST SHIP
WHEN LIFE'S SEAS BECOME STORMY.

THE FORWARD LOOK

...but this one thing I do,
forgetting those things which are behind, and
reaching forth unto those things which are before,
Philippians 3:13 (KJV)

I start this day with optimism / No place for pessimism / The clouds can't dull my drive / There's joy in being alive / Need to make the most of the occasion / Submit to God's persuasion / Acknowledge that this is my chance / Assume the faith stance / Must dig deep in belief / Conviction that brings relief / Riveted on the prize / Undaunted despite the size / Knowing that God does provide / Jehovah Jireh of life's tide / Determined to keep on track / Moving forward / No turning back / It's easier when You lead / You meet the need / It's wise to keep You in front / My help when words are sharp and blunt / Your strength does not wane / Your presence is my gain / Despite the struggle and strain / No rush to complain / The victory is within reach / Must hold on to what You teach / You promised to be help in trouble / Doubt can't burst my bubble / Success is my right / Morning waits after the night / Got incentive to hold my course / You are the power force / It's going to be my greatest time / Abundance showered in my prime / Blessings which are indescribable / It's Your love that's viable / I can embrace my good / Your grace is understood / You have opened the door / I'm shouting over what's in store / It's the wealth of Your love / Your input comes from above / Truly committed to Your calling / You're not into stalling / I am thrilled to walk the earth / I possess the truth of its worth /

KEEP YOUR FAITH IN "DRIVE".
YOU AVOID TRANSMISSION PROBLEMS.

YOU ARE A WINNER

But what things were gain to me, those I counted loss for Christ.

Yea doubtless, and I count all things but loss for the excellency of the knowledge of Christ Jesus my Lord: for whom I have suffered the loss of all things, and do count them but dung, that I may win Christ,
Philippians 3:7-8 (KJV)

It's all an attitude of mind / Belief is the real find / Put doubt to flight / Conviction wins the fight / Refuse to be hemmed in / You are designed to win / Failure is not your DNA / You are a winner all the way / Life is yours to possess / No problem when you are the best / Your fate is success bound / Faith in God is mighty sound / Called to the kingdom for this hour / No sweat - God has the power / It's knowing God is for you / His promises are never overdue / Just be about your goal / You have a leading role / It's doing His will / Obedience with zeal / Grab hold of your plan / Act like God's man / Nothing can stop your ascent / You have His consent / No performing with fear / There's comfort when God is near / Release for the increase / It's hesitation that must decrease / The world is your jewel / God's grace is your pull / You have it under control / His protection is on patrol / Stay cool as you advance / It's the Father's pleasure to enhance / It's yours for the taking / No place for faking / Reach for the medal / Keep pressing the pedal / You have the winner's style / The mark of God's child / No reason to drop out / Why fret and pout / Deception is the enemy's game / Trying to mess up your name / But you know who you are / You are God's star / Your reward is spiritual security / The sign of master maturity / That's why you can't lose / You exercised the power to choose / You made the wise choice / Counseled by the Lord's voice / No need to retreat / God can't be beat / It's a clear victory in view / Entrée on your menu / Get ready for the convocation / That's a great celebration / It's your ceremony / You denied the acrimony / You put God in your scheme / Way you won your dream / You are a success story / Discovered it was His glory / God gives you His stamp / Trusting Him is why you are champ /

YOU ARE A WINNER. PICK UP YOUR MEDAL!

THE FLAG

... and let his banner over me be love.
Song of Solomon 2:4 (NIV)

Some stick it on their cars / Stripes and the stars / Late discovery of its power / Symbol to sustain in grief's hour / Alright if you want to show the flag / But a hollow spirit is a "drag" / Need to do more than worship Old Glory / There's another side to the story / Flag ought to be a melting station/ Evidence that we are one nation / But looking at hatred and games we play / Means that flag has not helped our meanness to delay / Still see people judged by their skin / Badge that says – you can't come in / But we wave the flag / Saw that there was some profiling by police / People harassed and not released / We wave the flag / Put it on our lapel / Raise our voices and we yell / Yet there are some waiting with stories to tell / Don't want to hear any criticism / Speaking leads to ostracism / Now is the hour to sound the alarm / Easy patriotism can lead to harm / Loving our country is fine / It's abuse which dulls the shine / More to it than waving flags / Need something to inspire when hope lags / Flag waving is often an outside show / But inside is where honesty and integrity grow / Need is to challenge for deeper reflection / See if our flag waving can stand inspection / For it's not just what we display on our poles / Knowing how to help and love are real goals / So whether the flag flies in the breeze / Better to help each other – if you please / Fly the flag if we must / But live in a way that "It's in God we trust" / All will come out in the end / Just join in and let our faith blend / It's true without contradiction / Flag waving without love increases friction / Let it dance in the wind / Truth and honor will never offend /

NEVER DRAG THE FLAG IN
THE MUD OF OUR OWN SELFISHNESS

ENCOURAGE YOURSELF!

WHAT'S ON YOUR MIND

Study to shew thyself approved unto God, a workman that needeth not to be ashamed, rightly dividing the word of truth.
II Timothy 2:15 (KJV)

Big question on the table / Looking at life and not just cable / More to living than hanging out / Got to train for our bout / Not going to win out of shape / Can't ignore the tale of the tape / Getting fat on laziness / That's some kind of craziness / Growing crops of dumbness / Evidence of mental numbness / Got a chance to advance / More than sex and romance / Find something that will last / Passion and playing will soon pass / More than satisfying lust / Man, that's nothing to trust / God wants you to excel / Exceeding average and prevail / Challenges you to hear the call / Get up – stand tall / No more lying in the cut / Minds don't grow in a rut / The door is ajar / Open path to your star / Just start with assurance / God's breath aids the endurance / Success is no deception / Gear your attitude for right reception / The plan has no tricks / Do God's will despite the licks / For whatever comes your way / Can't be whipped if you don't delay / Face the challenge with pride / Stop cringing and don't hide / God will give you what you need / Follow Him and heed His lead / All things will come clear / Clouds fade when He's near / Trust not only in self / Doing that will put you on the shelf / Look to the Master's will / Start out and climb the hill / God gives zeal to close the deal / No longer vacillation and hibernation / It's time for manifestation / You stand as a champ in the ring / The God Hook-up is the real thing / Lift your voice and sing / Let your becoming take wing /

YOU CAN'T LOSE WHEN GOD IS YOUR CORNER MAN!

DON'T STOP

I have fought the good fight, I have finished the race, I have kept the faith.
II Timothy 4:7 (NIV)

Need to run with vision / Make the right decision / Refuse to be deterred / Going forward is preferred / Some don't understand why I won't retire / Truth is: I still got some fire / God has more for me to do / Raises me to a new view / Must keep my mind on point / Secure that He will anoint / Keeps me moving / Got to keep grooving / Temptation says quit / But I just can't sit / Got a task that demands grit / Meet confusion with wit / Not trapped in a snit / Respond to the duty at hand / Heed the Lord's command / Run and persevere / Hang in and stay sincere / Might look like a lost cause / Don't linger and pause / Mission must not be lost / Price of stopping is a heavy cost / Can't just meander like a fly / Need to be sharp and not sigh / Must stay alive / It's the season to thrive / The enemy wants me to stop / But I'm seeking the top / Really not going to turn around / Determined to cover the ground / And that's real sound / Will continue when trials hound / The trip is divine / Running for God is fine / It's a thing that's really hip / Trusting God so I won't slip / Know this for real / God's work is my meal / Jesus said it was meat / Ministry that's not all neat / But the joy is in striving /

Never ending but always arriving / Committed to the marathon run / ecstatic joy in hearing "Well Done." /

"GET UP AND LIVE."

COME ON PEOPLE

What shall we then say to these things? If God be for us, who can be against us?
Romans 8:31 (KJV)

Stop lying in your bed / Get up – can't play dead / Come on people / Stop your cowering / Opportunities are showering / Run and get the prize – that's really wise / No more talking / Let's get to walking / We have a world to build / We construct with visionary zeal / We know that we are a people of grace and beauty / Just keeping our history is our duty / We have fallen victim to the man's game / Scared to say who we are – that's our shame / Stop trying to "ape" what we ain't / We are a unique people who will not faint / Must not act like we are brand X / We are not going to just wait to be next / We shall mold new inventions / Got to have the right intention / Ignore convention and engage in death prevention / Come on people – death's more than a bullet that will kill / Death is assassination of the will / So believe in who we are / We always followed the North star / We saw our victory in the sky / Never giving up / Refusing to die / And so today, let's get it together / Don't come apart - beaten by a feather / We can do whatever we start / Just know that it's a matter of the heart / Come on people – we got a mission to achieve / Don't forget our destiny is what we believe / This is our day /

Let's affirm the way / God is on our side / No doubt that belief is the vehicle to ride / It's all in our hands / Just heed the truth commands / Come on people – it's in our court / We pay the price for selling ourselves short / Come on people / Climb the steeple /

STOP WHINING AND START DEFINING!

NOW IS THE TIME

for the time is at hand.
Revelation 22:10 (KJV)

Cannot run and hide / Now's the time to decide / Which way we must go / Get up and truth seeds sow / Lead others to a new stance / Boldly reach out and take a chance / Stop waiting for others to do / Using what's ours gives victory too / Look in the mirror and see / It's the picture of you and me / There is a real solution / Must evict mind pollution / Now is the time / Opportunity is knocking loud / Can't just get lost in a crowd / Got to push our way through / To our dreams and hopes be true / Wise up and know / Our moments come to glow and show / It's about finding new ground / Making plans that are strong and sound / Got a vision for this hour / Truth to be shouted from the village tower / Now's the time / Let the trumpet make its call / Standing up is growing tall / Not playing a fool's game / Looking for others to blame / Better to seize this hour / Brave souls don't bend and cower / Valiant spirits sound the alarm / Red alert to avert the storm / Playing with time is a real crime / Can't pretend that the clock won't chime / Truth is that the hand is moving / Can't linger when it's about proving / Let the plans get grooving / Time to do new things / Reach out and spread our wings / Can't just remain frozen / Seeking the summit is for the chosen / Now's the time / Make it sublime / Leave your mark on earth / Righteous payment for your birth / Releasing ideas to motivate / Bold projects that renovate / Dark rooms are in need of light / Illumined by those with fertile sight / Now's the time / The season is prime /

THIS IS YOUR PREGNANT MOMENT.
HOW'S YOUR PRENATAL CARE?

IT'S GOING ON

He put a new song in my mouth,
a hymn of praise to our God....
Psalm 40:3 (NIV)

Looking for some real action / Deep meaning and satisfaction / God's got it going on / Can turn noise to a mellow tone / His trust you can rely / Never leaves you to whine and sigh / He's going on / Right there when day is run / Not a fair weather friend / Sticks it out to the end / The Man's got it going on / Problems weigh a ton / Ain't got no fun / No heat from the sun / Feel like it's over and done / God is right on time / Doubting Him is capital crime / His act is super "bad" / Brings you through when things are sad / Tell you my God is "out of sight" / Always taking me to higher height / Feel like I'm ten feet tall / Know my God is best of them all / His way is the sure thing / His peace is the song I sing / This Lord is in charge / Handles the issue – no matter how large / He's really the Master Authority / His teaching is priority / Got to celebrate / His wisdom will renovate / God can mobilize my mission / Victory found in His permission / Not going to betray the King / His truth is the real thing / Yes, believe it and proclaim / Jehovah Elohim is the name / All life is enhanced / His program must be advanced / Have a smile on my face / Know that God is first place / Wake up all who are not wise /

God can realize and actualize / Put pep in your step / Glide in your stride / Gleam in your eye / No way you're gonna die / God's your ace in the hole / Badder than that – half has not been told / God's grace has more to unfold / More precious than platinum and gold / Got a right to talk loud / Inform the crowd / I'm truly having fun / God still ain't done / Never changes from rising to setting sun / God's got it going on / It's truth and not a con / God's got it going on /

GOD WILL TURN YOU ON. THERE'S NO OFF SWITCH!

I'M SO EXCITED

Nevertheless he left not himself without witness, in that he did good..., filling our hearts with ... gladness
Acts 14:17 (KJV)

My day is rich / Freed from a ditch / Jesus did it / There's no hitch / His love picked me up / Did indeed visit and sup / Guess it's all real / New life's in His will / I'm so excited / Path has been lighted / Got a song to share / The hymn says He does care / Didn't have to buy my case / Gave me amazing grace / Got a right to leap and shout / His truth is what it's about / Salvation brought me out / Saved a sinner / Made me a winner / Brings tears to my eyes / New life is the prize / Left the old game / That was a way of shame / No more blame / He came to offer direction / Change my projection / No more defection / Others got to know / My life's got a new glow / They can't believe I'm the same guy / Didn't care if I would live or die / Now it's all a thrill / Happy without a drink or pill / Jesus is the reason / Freed me from the winter season / Spring has entered my space / Excited about my place / No need to act cool / I'm a pupil in the Jesus school / Eager to study my lesson / Sure glad it's my blessing / No more wandering blind / I got Jesus on my mind / May seem small to you / But He brought me through / If you knew where I started / Didn't think my life could be charted / He rescued me from ignorance and pride / Like Abraham said, "The Lord will provide" / Part of His bumper crop / No longer a flop / Liberated from sin's stress / His love lifts me from mess / I'm so excited / I can jump and whirl / He's in charge of my world /

YOU OUGHT TO BECOME A LIVING TESTIMONY.
LOOK HOW FAR YOU HAVE COME.

GO DEEP

But God hath revealed them unto us by his Spirit: for the Spirit searcheth all things, yea, the deep things of God.
I Corinthians 2:10 (KJV)

Time to go deep / Wake up from foolish sleep / Waste of talent is sad / Messing around is really bad / Must move with a vision / Living wise is the right decision / Shallow schemes have little power / That's just pabulum for this hour / Need some deep stuff / Strength when it gets tough / Got to go deep / The Word must be reaped / Nothing is too hard if we believe / Faith will relieve / Doubt can't conceive / His promise won't deceive / Jesus is the Ideal Man / His life is a saving plan / He doesn't teach lying around / False path to winning a crown / Calls us to be aware / Promised His care to share / It's time for a new program / Guidance from the great "I AM" / No way we will flop / The Christ Mind lives at the top / Always operating for good / Bringing light to the "hood" / Jesus says, "Go deep" / No barrier we can't leap / Stand on His base / He's never lost a case / All things prosper in Him / Got our backs when chances look slim / We must go deep / Blown opportunity is a reason to weep / Jesus is the heavyweight champ / Laziness evicted from His camp / Time to go deep / Playing scared is cheap / Catching the ball in stride /

Winning through Jesus is Heaven's pride / Go deep and stay alert / Sharp minds never flirt / Kingdom is ours to possess / Don't take a foolish recess / This is the Lord's Word to us / His resumé is about trust / His game has no shame / We thrive in His name / Get on board / He's sharper than a two-edged sword / Winning souls for Christ / That's the truth of paradise / The Master has what we need / Sprinkles our ground with His seed / What a thrill to do His will / Make it to the top of the hill / Can lift our voices in song / No defeat for the God strong / Our charge is to never give up / We shall hold the victory cup / Go deep / Eternal joy is ours to keep /

JESUS IS THE QUARTERBACK.
HIS PASSES ARE PERFECT.

ALLERGIES

and give relief to you who are troubled,...
II Thessalonians 1:7 (NIV)

It's the season of sneezing / People coughing and wheezing / They say it's mold / That's what I've been told / Have to take an allergy shot / Get rid of what I got / Guess it does turn eyes red / Often feels like the walking dead / Tears running down our cheeks / Laid up for weeks / Shoot spray up our noses / Some say its pollen of roses / All I know for sure / No fun to endure/ It's a really bad time / Punished for no crime /Allergies are a worry / Need an answer in a hurry / But we keep on rehearsing the case / Experiencing its bad taste / Talk about finding a solution / Win a prize for resolution / Throat fighting its tickle / It's really a pickle/ Allergies don't need a reason / They just show up in season / Putting our days in strife / Nighttime is not the good life / It's what we contend / Must face it and not pretend / We would sing high praises / Just can't tolerate daisies / And so the tale unwinds / Hay fever strangles and binds / But you wonder why I write about this / I'll tell you after I spray my mist / You see – it's easier to reflect / When you don't have to disinfect / Can think deeper ideas / Not wiping away tears / Would like to engage in sublime meditation / Must fight the irritation / Know it's nothing new / Sure would enjoy not saying "achoo" / I really could go deep / I just need some sleep / Wish there were a better way / Refuse allergy its say / Would love to do imagination / My sinus is in agitation / I want to write and ponder / Allergies plot to take me under / This is my only reason / Tired of hacking and sneezing / Will soon return to issues more complex / It's when allergies end their hex. /

LET'S CALL FOR IMMUNITY IN THE COMMUNITY!
ALLERGY SUFFERERS OF THE WORLD: UNITE.

YOU ARE AWESOME

Dear Lord:

You are Awesome / You are Amazing / You are Assurance / You are Able / You are Accessible / You are Aware / You are Accomplished / You are Active / You are Abundant / You are Above / You are Accommodating / You are Accountable / You are Accurate / You are Actual / You are Adept / You are Adjacent / You are Adroit / You are Aerial / You are Affirmative / You are Affectionate / You are Affable / You are Afflicted / You are Affordable / You are Alliance / You are Alive / You are Ally / You are Allness / You are Amicable / You are Amnesty / You are Amenable / You are Approachable / You are Applicable / You are Approving / You are Appealing / You are Apparent / You are Appropriate / You are Ardent / You are Armed / You are Assertive / You are Astonishing / You are Assiduous / You are Attentive / You are Attached / You are Attractive/ You are Authority / You are Author/ You are Audible / You are Auspicious / You are Awoke / You are Axis/ You are Alpha!

Amen

BIOGRAPHY

REVEREND HENRY O. HARDY was called to pastor Chicago's historic Cosmopolitan Community Church in 1967 and served faithfully for 47 years. A graduate of the University of Illinois School of Journalism. Reverend Hardy received a Bachelor of Divinity from the University of Chicago Divinity School. He also earned a Masters of Arts Degree in Theology and Literary Criticism from the University of Chicago.

Among his many awards and special merits, Reverend Hardy was awarded an Honorary Doctorate of Divinity Degree by the G.M.O.

Throughout his years of preaching, teaching and reaching, Reverend Hardy is well known for taking his ministry to the streets – into the bristling heart of the urban community. As chairman of the PUSH-CBS Negotiation Team, Reverend Hardy had the responsibility of apprising the media of the concerns of minorities. Special interest was programming, fairness in equity, and parity in hiring and decision-making in addition to key concerns involving banking in minority owned banks, and the use of minority products and services.

A much sought-after lecturer and public speaker, Reverend Hardy has spoken at colleges, universities, schools, churches across the United States and abroad.

He was a featured speaker at the historic Million Man March in Washington, D.C.

Reverend Hardy, a former journalist, has written for the St. Louis Argus, Chicago Defender, and Gary American newspapers.

Reverend Hardy's community affiliations include:

Board Member, Broadcast Ministers Alliance, DuSable Museum of African-American History; Sigma Delta Chi (Professional Journalism Fraternity); Alpha Phi Alpha Fraternity; Board Member, Church Federation of Greater Chicago; Board Member, Young Men's Christian Association; Board Member, One Church/One Child; Former Second Vice President, South Side Branch of the N.A.A.C.P; Executive Committee, Concerned Citizens for Police Reform; Board Member of Operation P.U.S.H. Reverend Hardy, for many years was "The Voice of P.U.S.H." where he served as the anchor for the weekly radio broadcast.

Reverend Hardy is the recipient of numerous awards and has been the subject of newspaper and magazine articles. He is the recipient of the "2003 Gospel Supreme Labor of Love Award" and has also appeared as a guest on several television programs.

Reverend Hardy has lectured at the following colleges and universities:

Fisk University – Nashville, Tennessee;

University of Chicago – Chicago, Illinois

University of Illinois Chicago Circle Campus – Chicago, Illinois;

University of Illinois Champaign - Urbana Campus – Champaign, Illinois;

Benedict College – Columbia, South Carolina;

Triton College – River Grove, Illinois;

Lewis University – Lockport, Illinois;

Michigan State University – Michigan, Illinois;

William Jewell College – Liberty, Missouri; and

McKendree University – Lebanon, Illinois.

His many accomplishments include: creation of the Cosmopolitan Consciousness Experience – a teaching and motivational class relating the Bible to 21st Century Christian Living; creator of the "Voice of Cosmopolitan" radio ministry; Founder of Cosmopolitan's Institute for Creative and Positive Living (ICPL), and originator of "Dynamic Living" TV Ministry.

Other achievements include:

Co-Host: "Terry's Tempel" – Local Talk Show
Co-Host: "Spiritual Alternative" – Local Radio TV Talk Show
Chicago, Illinois

Featured Ecumenical Keynote Speaker
National Convention – Alpha Phi Alpha
Washington, D.C.

Keynote Speaker:

City-Wide Dr. Martin Luther King, Jr. Observance
Columbus, Georgia

Featured Speaker at the World Conference of Mayors
Monrovia, Liberia

He is the author of BECOMING, a collection of essays and meditation.

He is currently planning for completion of a forthcoming book.

978-0-9915335-6-5
Pastor Henry O. Hardy
BECOMING
transformative . informative . restorative
WWW.MCCLUREPUBLISHING.COM
McClure Publishing

www.ingramcontent.com/pod-product-compliance
Lightning Source LLC
Chambersburg PA
CBHW070542010526
44118CB00012B/1185
9780998922355